Christ Church, Frederica
St. Simons Island, Georgia

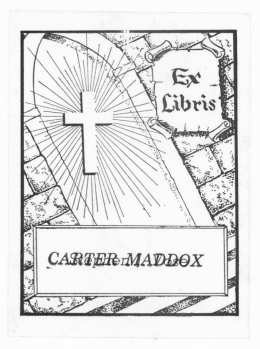

Ex Libris

CARTER MADDOX

A Testament of Turning

A Testament

By
DONET MEYNELL ROELOFS

of Turning

MOREHOUSE-BARLOW CO.
New York

PRINTED IN THE UNITED STATES OF AMERICA

To the glory of God
and in memory of my mother,
Mildred Seyster Sorensen

Foreword

An admired and beloved friend is coming to see me. Some of his time I would keep to myself; but I should be an unusual person if I did not want to present him to my friends and share him with them. Perhaps this simple analogy may offer some clue to the continuing presentation of books about religion. Certainly it is a fact that if we know something about God and particularly if we know Him in some fashion for ourselves, we must share this knowledge. All religious history bears testimony to this human trait.

Yet it is not merely a pattern of our making. The necessity to make known what He has revealed to us is part of the record and of the very experience itself. Our need to go, to tell, is not our device, but His command. It is His idea far more than ours. We may act unwillingly like Moses, or as men under authority, like the Eleven, or with a sort of joyful compulsion like St. Paul's "woe is me if I preach not the gospel." But we know that to see and hear requires that we pass on what He has given us.

The literature of religion also indicates that God is never monotonous. The description of His way with His children varies with each one who records it. Books about religion can often be rather dull; but the account of how He has dealt with us, written from experience, is frequently fascinating and almost inevitably new. The value of such records to the reader is primarily the discovery of what God does for men if we will open the door, and the growing conviction that whatever our unique difficulties may be He can and does lead us to an ever greater knowledge of Himself.

So I am happy to add a Foreword for this book, in the hope that what God has done in and with its author may encourage others who share some of the problems she faced to "stop, look, and listen" to the Holy Spirit who would lead them also into the firsthand knowledge of the family of God. For each of us the point of origin will be unique; for each of us the road will vary; but there is a Way and a Guide, and there is truly a Home and a welcome.

WILLIAM F. LEWIS
Bishop of Olympia

Preface

The following is a series of actual letters, written to various friends and relatives in my search for God. I never intended to do anything with them until last year when my Bishop, the Rt. Rev. William F. Lewis, Bishop of Olympia (then Bishop of Nevada), encouraged me to think in terms of publication. Some months later I began to plan seriously to submit my letters for publication in the form of a book.

My only excuse for this is that when I was a skeptic, an unbeliever, and floundering about, I was sometimes irritated by books written from a "finished" point of view. I used to protest when an author availed himself of such hindsight, "It's all very well for you who have 'arrived,' so to speak; but what about me—with my rational reservations, my emotional biases?" For the agnostic, belief is never quite so simple as it is made out to be. Consequently, I always found more nourishment in those books which were written out of the author's own experience—and they are very few in number. I hope this book will be at least cheering to those who are seeking to find God, to those who are in darkness and confusion.

However, this is not for those who wish a technical treatise on religion, a knowledgeable discussion of theology or the doctrines of the Church. There are many excellent books available on these subjects, written by experts. The only thing I claim to know anything about is the experience of the beginner and the difficulties he encounters in coming to

9

belief—and the rich rewards of a well-grounded faith. Here I deal with the perennial questions: Is there a God? How and where can we find Him? Wherever references are made to religious writings, they are made not so much to instruct the reader as to clarify my own experience.

I am chiefly indebted to Bishop Lewis for fostering my book and helping to bring it to fruition. I am also most grateful to my neighbor, Priscilla Manspeaker, for serving as a sounding board. Madaline Roseman, Sister Magdala, the Rev. T. H. Kerstetter, and my husband, Robert Roelofs, were especially generous with their time and suggestions. Above all, I am beholden to the people to whom these letters were written, who were the midwives to the new life I entered into, at first so unwillingly.

My experiences as set down here are creative, as are all our dealings with God, but they are not unique. It is impossible to be original in any religious undertaking. We find that what we think we have discovered all by ourselves is what many others have discovered before us. So it is with every aspect of our life: going off to school, falling in love, getting married, bearing children, losing a loved one, facing the end of our life. It is both humbling and reassuring to learn that what we thought was so novel and so individual is but the shared experience of all mankind. But how exciting to find that we also have this common heritage in our relationship with God!

If you are complacent in your present convictions, or if you have a closed mind about religious experience, this book is not for you. Nor is it if you are certain there is no God, or do not care one way or another. But if you are beginning to have the uneasy feeling that there may be a world of Reality beyond the wall of your commonplace experience; if, perhaps, you have from time to time glimpsed the grapes of glory clustering on the vine, just out of sight and out of reach; if you have outgrown your faith and want to start on a perilous adventure into the vast country of God's love, then these letters may assist you in that high venture.

D.M.R.

Contents

I. LETTER TO UNCLE FRANK 17
    Wherein I start my search for God; I make inquiries and examine the evidence; I come to love Him before I can believe in Him.

II. LETTER TO SARA 37
    I am filled with doubts about becoming confirmed; I re-examine the rational and psychological grounds for my belief; I capitulate—more through love than reason.

III. LETTER TO MILTON 56
    I express some of my confusion; I protest leaving my Mother Church; I cannot believe I can find God in Nevada.

IV. LETTER TO MADALINE 63
    I make my first attempt to answer someone else's questions about God: namely, how we come to know Him.

V. LETTER TO BISHOP LEWIS 71
    I encounter my first barren period; I am separated from God and my faith is shaken; I learn that emotion is not a trustworthy guide; I am restored to God through a mystical experience.

VI. LETTER TO SISTER VERONICA   89

*I have started reading the lives of the saints and
am cheered by finding a common core of Christian experience.*

VII. LETTER TO HUGH   110

*I try to acquire virtue and get bogged down and
discouraged; I am beginning to discover that the
things I learn will not stay learned.*

VIII. LETTER TO MY RELATIVES   135

*I tell of my mother's death; I learn how to make
a full submission of my will to God; I also learn
I no longer have to escape from reality.*

IX. LETTER TO BOB   146

I take up the problem of evil and pain.

X. LETTER TO SVEN   168

*I try to define wherein Christianity lies for a
skeptic who protests that it isn't realistic.*

XI. LETTER TO PRISCILLA   186

*I pass on to my neighbor my impressions of a
visit to a religious community; I also learn something of physical suffering.*

XII. LETTER TO FATHER TED   200

*I bring my experiences up to date and draw
some conclusions about the religious life.*

ACKNOWLEDGMENTS   217

A Testament of Turning

I shall not live
            till I see God;
and when I have seen Him
            I shall never die.
                        —*John Donne*

I

Letter to Uncle Frank

Atlanta, Georgia
June 3, 1955

Dear Uncle Frank:

You will be surprised at hearing from me—after all these years of nothing but Christmas cards and birth announcements. You will be even more surprised to hear that I've made a decision about something. I think I would like to find out if there is a God and, if there is, if I might establish any kind of relationship with Him.

It is curious that in my search I would think of turning first to you. Although you are my husband's uncle and I have met you only once, in this matter I feel closer to you than to anyone else. I suppose this is because you were the first person I ever talked with about God.

I remember so vividly when I met you, when Bob and I came to visit you on Long Island. We visited the monastery, where you lived as a brother and a priest, and then stopped in at St. Anne's. I remember thinking it was a charming little church, and that the monastery was forbidding. I thought it was curious that a monk could have a sense of humor, but I also thought you must be a little daft to be attracted to such a life. I dismissed practically everything you said to me, not sneeringly, but simply because it seemed to have nothing to do with me. But you planted a seed of doubt in me that has,

17

for some reason, begun to grow and is about to wrench my mind apart.

If I, too, am to become daft and succumb to what I have for so long viewed as the sickness of religion, I want to know what I'm letting myself in for. I remember your saying that man was incurably religious. I'm beginning to believe that you may be right!

When we visited you five years ago I experienced a little prick of curiosity, followed by a vague hunger that gnawed at me from time to time. I set this down to frustrated mother-love. So, shortly after we returned to New Haven, I decided to stop all the nonsense about waiting to be able to afford our children, and soon afterwards Meredith was on the way. We lost one baby after Meredith, and then last year Mark was born. Now I have two delightful children, but my hunger remains; it refuses to be sublimated entirely in parental love.

A year and a half ago I learned that at Emory University psychotherapy was available to all members of the faculty and their families free of charge. So I proceeded to take advantage of it, much as a woman will swoop down upon a bargain whether or not she needs it, simply because it's cut-rate. I soon learned that I could benefit from therapy in many ways and, also, that it was not going to be quite the lark I had supposed. Then I thought, well, this hunger is due to my immaturity. I figured that once I was all normalized and grown up I would lose that craving. Instead, to my growing uneasiness, I found its pulse beating more strongly; I found that down in the midst of me, in the core of my personality, at unfathomable depths, there was a restlessness, an insatiable curiosity, a driving need to believe in and find God.

Now I feel free enough to try. Before, I was bound unto myself; now I am released—in all directions—toward myself, toward people, and toward the mysteries at the heart of things. I almost feel as if I could become a poet again!

It's not only this, though, a desire to believe in something, an intellectual curiosity, it's——? No, I can't put my finger on it. But now I am no longer afraid of being hurt, not even in my relationships with people. It is curious: now that I am unarmed, vulnerable, bringing my heart in my hands, why should it be only now that I can go unafraid, being able to absorb the unexpected hurt into myself? Is that the way I was with God? Afraid to search lest I could not find Him? Fearful of disappointment, rebuff, negation? Yes, I think that was it, or part of it. And I must, realistically, be prepared for it without being dismayed by it.

Still, I want to do it. I never have, really. I can take no stand, I have no convictions one way or another, about so many things. And that isn't being very honest. People all about me believe in things that seem utterly inane. They believe in a God who made heaven and earth, in a God-man who atoned for us. Or they believe in Harmony as a supreme value. They believe in a series of infinitesimally small accidents or mutations which brought this and other worlds into existence. They believe in each other, or disbelieve in each other, on no grounds at all. They believe in the most ridiculous and untenable things and for no good reason at all—that I can see.

But I can't go on all my life not knowing why I can't believe in God, in Harmony, in accidents, in people. I have to know one way or another, or at least to know that it isn't possible to know one way or another. All I can say now is that I don't think it's possible, it doesn't seem likely that we can know; but I've never tried, I've never without bias honestly undertaken such a search.

Very well. Where does one go from here? I can't go to a clergyman because I don't belong to any Church.* Oh, I was baptized in one, but I'm farther from that in my heart than I am in time. I can't go to the representatives of Harmony, Beauty, Love, Metaphysical Unity, or Cosmic Accident because they aren't organized; they have no offices or licensed spokesmen. I can't even go to people, random friends, and ask them why they believe what they believe, because they don't seem to know. Even if they did know, it wouldn't be of any help because their answers would be their answers, not mine. Furthermore, there's no point in reading (at least not at this juncture); that's something I've done all my life. If all my schooling, an M.A. in Philosophy, and the perusal of dozens of books on the subject haven't clarified matters for me, I see no reason to suppose they will at this point.†

Perhaps I need to get acquainted with some religious people. But I doubt if that would help, any more than a lifetime of contact with human beings was able to make me into one. It wasn't until therapy, a traumatic experience dealing with the mechanics of becoming a human being, that I made some real progress here. So it would seem that I need some

---

* This I learned later was not so much because of lack of Church affiliation as it was due to a disinclination to be proselytized. Such a feeling I soon discovered was unwarranted—at least in connection with the priests I encountered.

† The books were, however, largely on the subject of philosophy, not on religion as such. I have come to see that for me, at any rate, books on religion, particularly those written not on a theoretical level, but out of the writer's own experience, have been especially helpful. Those written from a philosophical point of view are second order, twice removed, and do not impel me to action. If it can be said that the testimony of the expert is invaluable in other fields, why should it not be so here? Consequently, I feel it is not the polemics of the scholars, but the witness of the disciples, the early Church Fathers, the saints of all ages, the members of the vast family of God who can best instruct us.

kind of experience in relation to universal values, whether divine, human, or natural. But how does one set such an experience into motion when one doesn't know wherein it lies?

You see, there are grave difficulties even before I begin. But I'll never have such an opportunity again: to see nature clear-eyed and untrammeled by theories, opinions, doctrines.

I promise myself one thing: I will never accept any conclusion until it has been tested by experience, nor will I admit anything to credence until it has been examined to the fullest extent of my intelligence. However, I will not insist that the reverse be true: that experience, to be valid, must be understood. It isn't in other areas of life, so why must it be here? Of course, this may be quite different; perhaps still other principles are involved here—that is what is to be discovered. But I do believe (ah, I believe something!) that the ultimate values of life, while they may be beyond the ken of my mind, are not by their nature at odds with it, that it is not only fitting but urgent and necessary that I bring to bear all of my capacities in this venture.

It's really quite exciting to set out on such an uncharted course. It's entirely possible that, like Columbus, I may find quite inadvertently an entirely new land. One thing is certain: anything is possible. In any event I can't stay here. The values of my life have become too narrow for the kind of person I'm coming to be.

June 14, 1955

Becalmed. No wind at my back and all the sails hang limp. My pen won't work and it's devilishly hot in Atlanta. However, I've thought a great deal about what my first step might be and it occurs to me that, although I might not recognize it, the Lutheran Church, in which I chose to be baptized and confirmed at the age of thirteen, might consider itself to have some spiritual claim on me. That tie must be broken at once. I had thought I might wait until I could come to some decision about matters before I cut myself asunder. But it doesn't seem likely that I'll end up as a member of any Church, so why continue to maintain a tie that has no meaning for me? This is not the kind of honesty I promised myself. I know, however, that it is impossible for me to return to the Lutheran Church—I outgrew that nearly twenty years ago. I'll write to Pastor Claus in the morning. At least it is one action I can take in a becalmed sea.

June 16, 1955

I did a curious thing today—experimentally, you might say. Instead of writing at once to my pastor I went to see a Lutheran minister in Atlanta and asked to be given a private Communion. I told him I was planning to drop my Lutheran membership and that, before I did, I wished to receive Communion. He seemed to see nothing strange in this, although I neglected to mention to him that I didn't believe in God. According to a few passages I remember from the Lutheran Communion service this automatically damns me to hell. Fortunately, I don't believe this.

Yet in what sense *did* I believe I would receive any benefits from partaking of Holy Communion when I was not only not in a state of grace, but not even sure of the existence of God? My act was largely symbolic. Naturally, it had nothing to do with the main import of the Communion service, with Christ's Body and Blood. Perhaps I felt that, by involving myself again in the Sacrament, I was telling God that, if

He existed, I wanted to find Him. It was rather like a challenge; since I couldn't pray, it was the best way I knew of approaching Him. As a Christian, you will undoubtedly be shocked by this*—not only by my act but by my attitude. Believe me, for me this is the height of humility!

For some reason, however, my sacrilege made me feel uncommonly good and, filled with resolve, as if I had somehow broken into an unyielding circle, I dashed off to write my letter. The wind was in my sails and I was off. I knew exactly what I wanted to do next.

So by an act of thievery, one might call it, my journey into the void begins.

July 20, 1955

I have started instruction with a Roman Catholic priest. I have always had a very strong feeling that I belonged in the Catholic tradition. That is partly why the Lutheran Church originally attracted me, because of its liturgical form of service. Robert would split a gusset if I ever did join the Roman Church, but it's not very likely that I will, so I'm not going to be too concerned about that now. However, I think I owe

---

* From my present vantage point it shocks me, too. I now believe that the Church is right in defending the sanctity of this Sacrament against experiments or flippancy. In the present controversy over whether Communion should be open to all baptized persons whatever their persuasion, I will not take sides. I do feel, however, that if a person has no convictions as to the Real Presence of our Lord in the Sacrament, it is a meaningless act at the very least —and meaninglessness does not belong in an act of faith that is so meaningful. For example, we should not expect to be invited into the special practices or the sacred rites of a lodge meeting unless we were initiated members of such an organization. How much more has the Church a right to restrict participation in the holiest of all her Sacraments to those who are members of Christ and have some understanding of its nature.

it to myself to find out all I can about Catholic tradition.

In the meantime, while I was downtown hunting for a copy-writing job, I stopped in at one of the Episcopal churches —All Saints', I believe it's called. It's quite large, old, and æsthetically warm. I knelt down and, still unable to pray, listened to someone practising on the organ. I began to think about prayer and wondered how anyone could seriously believe he was communicating with a supernatural power. "Prophesy unto the wind,"[1] the Prophet cried, and if I could speak to God wouldn't I be doing the same thing as a man who calls out into a gale or runs his hand through a moving stream? To me, everything "out there" seemed as unstable as the very molecules in wind and water—and yet, I'm told, they are not unstable.

I fingered the Prayer Books standing in the racks and wondered if they contained meaning for people. How could they ever come to have any significance for me? Then I decided that the only thing to do was to find out if they could. I'll start attending Church services and see. I'll sample several Episcopal and several Roman churches, and tomorrow I'll go to see a rabbi for good measure.

July 21, 1955

And so I did! Rabbi Rothschild and I had a remarkable talk. It was helpful in many ways: first, it gave me a greater insight into his religion; and secondly, not being a Christian, he provided me with a neutral field into which I could pour my doubts and antipathies toward Christianity. I found I'd accumulated a sizable number. I found myself telling him

---

[1] References to numbered footnotes will be found in the Acknowledgments section beginning on page 217.

that sermons bored me, that piety seemed to me an abomination, that religion itself really looked like a kind of perfected and formalized escape mechanism. But I was forced back again to an unwilling conclusion that Christianity, whatever its faults, was something personable and alive and sound. Judaism has for me little advantage over the kind of working humanism I've been using for the last fifteen years, and it seems to embrace a cultural tradition in which I have no part. Guess I'll go look up some of my atheist friends and see how they're faring. It will give me contrast values, if nothing else. I wonder, really, what it would be like not to be so driven; to be able to accept beauty, friends, children, love, nature—without asking any questions. A much happier state of affairs, I'm sure; but I'm starting with one "given"—myself—and it doesn't seem to be in my nature to let things rest as they are.

September 2, 1955

Oh, good heavens, this will never do! By now I've attended over a half dozen Church services, Episcopal and Roman, and I'm completely at sea. Take the Episcopal services, for example—I feel as if I've wandered into a set for the Sadler's Wells ballet. After I've been ushered to a pew, vaguely feeling as if I ought to have a ticket, the woman in front of me drops into a kind of *plié* which I've learned is called a "genuflection." It throws me back on my heels a little and I collide with the person behind me who apparently does not do the same. We get all settled, though, when everyone falls forward, as at a given signal, onto the kneeling benches. Everyone seems prepared for it except me. I have purse, gloves, and a service sheet in my lap but I have to find a place for them before I can do anything. When everything has been dispensed with and I, too, am free to kneel, the organ shifts into open *diapason* and the congregation is on its feet for the "processional." I locate the hymn about the time the choir reaches the choir stalls.

From there things take off into something that's not even remotely familiar. Someone thrusts a Prayer Book into my hand, but by then I am two pages behind; I get caught up just as they all fall to their knees again. I have two policies, neither of which is wholly successful: either I must concentrate on the kneeling-sitting-rising continuum, or I must keep up with where they are in the Prayer Book. I honestly wonder if anyone ever has any time to concentrate on what is being said. Once I actually got actions one and two coordinated for a brief period until, bedizened with success, I dropped everything! I think it's impossible to become adjusted until the sermon, but by then I am so limp from my efforts that my mind wanders off to the pot roast.

I could simply sit and observe, I suppose, but that seems rather dull and I don't see how any of this is going to become *my* experience unless I learn how to participate. It doesn't seem likely that any of this has anything to do with God, but perhaps it does. The only questions I seem to come up with so far are: Why do people cross themselves, bow, genuflect, and when? The forms of the service, although foreign to me, are quite fascinating. I think I'm afraid to ask myself, let alone anyone else, any more questions. I'm bewildered, but for now I prefer to *stay* bewildered. I feel as if I'd been assaulted, and I think I'll retire to a quiet place for rumination and licking of wounds. After all, this—after fifteen years of not ever having been in a church—might lead to God knows what aberrations!

As for Christians themselves, as a group, they don't seem to carry any outstanding or distinguishing characteristics. Of course, I haven't had a close look at their private lives. Still, if I had the Power behind the universe behind *me*, I would think that I would generate something that would be obvious even to strangers. Perhaps not. Perhaps I have the wrong idea about God altogether. Yet it's repeatedly claimed that there is no difference that does not make a difference, and "by their fruits . . ." and all that. Well, if it doesn't make a difference it's not for me. However, I have to remind myself that I claim to have been changed significantly since psychotherapy; would any stranger, from casual observation of my behavior during a given period of time, be able to discern that change?

Wherein does it lie, then? What constitutes the difference between a Christian and a non-Christian? Apparently not in "churchmanship," as I believe it's called, in knowing when to do what during a service. All of that is quite obviously a symbolic means to a spiritual end, but apparently not in dramatic evidence in the people themselves. What *is* the end, the aim, the goal? It begins to look excessively intangible. I suppose it has something to do with the satisfaction of desire, just as, for no good reason that I can see, I harbor a desire to believe in God. There is a questionable argument abroad that man does not have a desire for that which does not exist. I have a good deal more respect for the scope of man's imagination than that! It seems much more reasonable to suppose that there are lacks, insufficiencies, in man that require fulfillment and support.* So maybe I *do* need a father-figure, or perhaps I still want to return to the womb; on the one hand a craving for authority, on the other a longing for a primitive kind of

---

* Later I came to accept this argument as pragmatically sound. The fact that our "lacks" and "insufficiencies" are met in God, the fact that we are unable, literally, to imagine anything that is not compounded of ideas arising out of our own experience—all this at least gives weight to the argument.

dependency. And it is less embarrassing to have an answer for unanswerable questions. This gets pretty subjective.

Assuming all this is true (and I think it is for many people), it would seem that Christianity requires something quite sizable by way of return: an unstinting giving of one's self, obedience, capacity for love, patience, self-control. These are very mature traits. I'm sure I'm not yet capable of them in any large measure. So, leaving aside neurotic escapism for the moment, what *can* bring forth all this? What is God? Where? How does He reveal Himself? Presumably He is more than just the Creator in an historical sense. Presumably He operates now, in the lives of His people. Where is the evidence?

I guess I'm ready to ask some questions, after all. But before I try to ascertain the attributes of religion, I had better first see if it has any objective validity. Does God, then, exist?

October 4, 1955

I have been considering some of the classical proofs for the existence of God, as represented by St. Thomas Aquinas, for example. It seems to me that all such proofs can be rationally compelling only when you grant the primary premises —which themselves cannot be proved and are not self-evident. The "proof" is thus limited to an enclosed system and has only epistemological significance. It tells us more about man and the process of his reasoning than it does about God. It leads us to further speculation, but not to absolute certainty. How can we presume to demonstrate God within the confines of our own reason? Of course, reason, if it cannot prove the existence of God, can certainly not disprove it. However, to posit these assumptions merely to avoid skepticism or to salvage our pygmy pride is not warranted. When I said earlier that I did not expect to find that God would be at odds with man's reason, I did not mean that man's reason could be made the measure of God.

There are other modern and more dynamic arguments which avoid the weakness of the Scholastics and do provide room for new evidence from modern science. While these later "open-ended" approaches do not provide coercive evidence, they do lead to a kind of circumstantial evidence that is intriguing. Since this is enough for our judicial system it ought to be enough for me! But it isn't; perhaps because I don't have sufficient awe of scientific method: I see through its hide to the bare bones of its logic. Any attempt at verification reveals a disjointed vertebra.

How, then, can I believe in God if I find rational arguments untenable? Is there any other evidence? What about emotion—can it be considered a proper basis for theological argument? William James tells us that if no hypothesis is backed by sufficient evidence, we do, nevertheless, have the right to believe on pragmatic grounds; but that reduces religion to a form of therapy dictated by need. James claims we have a right to exercise what he calls our "passional" nature. We can believe in God, essentially, because we want to. Does not that, too, make man the measure of God and, in this case, on psychological rather than rational grounds? But if we believe on insufficient evidence, even though this belief be true, are we not being dishonest? I think so.

I cannot accept the so-called "proofs" for the existence of God, nor can I believe simply to justify my desire. Is this, then, the end of the matter? Somehow I don't think so. I feel that there is further evidence that is better placed. As yet I cannot say in what this might consist, but it is imperative to find it if such evidence exists. I do not believe, with the skeptic, that it is better to risk the loss of truth than the chance of error.

November 6, 1955

I have found it necessary to eliminate the idea of becoming a Roman Catholic. I thought I would make such a good one, but now I find I wouldn't qualify at all—at least not at this time.

There are various reasons for thinking so: first of all, the Roman Church emphasizes the rational basis of belief, even the intellectual, for a person like me. While I am sure that reason plays a legitimate part in doctrine and belief, still I cannot be a part of a denomination whose *sine qua non* is founded almost exclusively on reason and logical proof, having discovered that I cannot on those very grounds convince myself of the existence of God.

Then there are other reservations. For one, I would probably have difficulty accepting Papal supremacy. If I am to accept the Biblical account I must agree that the Church was founded on the "rock"—but the word "rock" here does not refer to Peter as a person (that would be *Petros*); it is, rather, the Greek word *petra*, which refers to Peter's affirmation of Jesus' divinity when he proclaimed, "Thou art the Christ, the Son of the living God."[2] The Church is founded upon the witness of all the Apostles beginning with Peter, because he was the first to confess this rocklike truth which has held steady throughout the generations. The apostolic succession is based on this first confession of faith and is not confined to one and only one branch of the Holy Catholic Church. Nor could I accept the infallibility of Papal pronouncements.

Another point I would have difficulty with is the system of indulgences; here I would have to throw in my lot with Luther. I feel that judgment and mercy in this area are in God's hands, not man's, and that, unlike the Sacraments, this practice has no Scriptural basis. If not liable to misuse, it could easily foster a sort of utilitarianism in which God is "used" to further our salvation, not through a plan of redemption, but through a prudent manipulation of good works.

However, my chief objection is that in the Roman Catholic Church there is not enough participation on the part of the congregation. It seems to me that the liturgy of the Church should be in the language of its people and that the laity as well as the clergy should contribute to the fullest in worship and praise—in song, response, and prayer. Where the layman does not have full stature he loses a good deal of freedom; he is not at liberty to deal with the unknowns on his own, apart from dogmatic authority. This simplifies his responsibilities but does not allow enough room for growth.*

I should like to add that this is an individual choice and is not designed to influence others—merely to explain my own course of action. For those who are not handicapped by the demands of my mind and my personality the conclusions may be quite different. In any event, I am grateful for the opportunity of investigation; it has helped me rid myself of a few Protestant biases about the Roman Church, and what I have learned will not only enrich but influence my eventual choice —if, to be sure, I am going to be able to make one.

Now that I've decided not to go along with the Roman

* Here I am not speaking of matters of creed or basic doctrine: if there is a body of truth then it should be strictly maintained. I am referring to those questions that cannot be resolved on the basis of Scripture.

Church I feel both relieved and bereft. It seems hardly more likely that I will be able to accept the tenets and the doctrines of the Episcopal Church, since it is similar but with a different approach and emphasis, and it has a Protestant as well as a Catholic tradition. An appointment with the rector of All Saints' hasn't done much except to strengthen me in the conviction that there's very little of the basic doctrine of the Church that I can find acceptable, reasonable, or credible.

At least this relieves my mind of one suspicion: that in the Episcopal Church one can believe more or less what one wants to, and that the tenets of the Church are conveniently altered to suit the capacities and temperament of the customer. Just as I had had some groundless prejudices about the Roman Church, so I had a sort of vague impression that the Episcopal Church was a kind of glorified Unitarian sect, humanism frosted with ceremonial, catering largely to the carriage trade. While attendance in church is not dependent on what one can bring one's self to believe, membership and participation in the Sacraments are.

And that lets me out. This satisfies me; for if it were otherwise I would suspect there was no truth behind it. The kind of Truth I am seeking is not relative, is not adaptable to the whims of the individual. I am beginning to see what God is not; what He is, I have yet to discover.

November 15, 1955

Prayer is now possible for me. You will ask me how this came about, and I will not be able to tell you. I simply do not know. It's not a matter of taking certain steps or following anyone's advice, or pursuing a formula. It is more like being able to respond to a piece of music which was formerly ob-

scure and unyielding, and discovering that the obscurity and
the unyieldingness lay not in the music but in one's self.

Ever since I started attending church I have joined in the
communal prayers, although for the most part it was a stilted
performance. Private prayer remained abortive and self-conscious and rather like making a recording on a machine that
wasn't turned on. I have absolutely no rational grounds upon
which I can now assume that prayer has any reality, but
somewhere along the line a little "willing suspension of disbelief" seems necessary.

December 3, 1955

It is the first Sunday in Advent—a wonderful season of
expectation and mystery.

So many people are happily preparing for Christmastide,
as if indeed there were more behind the drama than the Yule
log and a tree decked with sparkle and light. During the last
couple of months it has become so necessary for me to believe—and so impossible—that I am filled with a torment and
a misery that far surpasses what I went through in therapy.
That was something of a game I was playing, a role that was
superimposed upon myself, assumed in order to bring about
certain difficult changes. This is far more real. It pervades
me and changes without changing; it requires something of
me that I am incapable of; it demands a response I cannot
give.

I wish I had known last summer that I was starting on
such a strange and terrible journey. What difference would
it have made if I had known? Would I have turned back?

The fact remains that I did not know in what my search
would consist. I suppose—it's hard to remember—I thought I

33

would try to see where I stood in regard to God and, if I could see my way clear to accept the doctrine of the Church, I would eventually join it and then my doubts and divisions would be at an end. But I soon found I couldn't do that, or I wasn't allowed to; at any rate it's fortunate that I couldn't, because if I had been able to accept God blindly it wouldn't have had much to do with me. It would have been a credo in someone else's name, not mine.

Yet all this time I honestly felt it behooved me to acquire acceptance in full measure and as rapidly as possible. I seemed impelled toward belief. Impatiently and anxiously I tried. Belief! Faith! I thought how simple and effortless it seemed for others, but how difficult for me. I thought how I envied those who had been born in the Church and could take it for granted, who did not have to learn how to know God. Or those who underwent conversion and, in a glorious and blinding step, pivoted upon themselves—while I, like a mole, must burrow my tedious and awkward way underground.

Can I now turn back? Oh, I want to so very much. I didn't know what I was getting into. It is not for the faint-hearted —and I am all of that. I simply don't have the courage or the perseverance or the strength. I've been fighting God every step of the way; from the very first "challenge," as I called it, in receiving Communion from the hands of a Lutheran pastor. I felt as if I had laid down an ultimatum: God, prove Yourself to me. And now I am being torn apart by the combat, the process of proof.

Oh, but I cannot stop now, as long as there is the faintest possibility that this is what it seems to be, a contest with Almighty God!

Christmas is over and I am thankful, exhausted by the strain and still not permitted to rest. I stayed away from the midnight celebration of Holy Communion on Christmas Eve simply because I was afraid. I could not face it. Instead I watched it on TV, from All Saints' Church, reasoning (quite laughably!) that it would thus reach me second-hand, so to speak, strained and enfeebled by distance, a picture of a picture. I was mistaken. It was very real, and I was in tears before it was over. I begin to see how Francis Thompson must have felt—pursued by the Hound of Heaven.

And yet I am still in flight. What is possible at this point? I must move cautiously. I cannot let my emotions lead me to unwarranted conclusions. I begin to sound like the man who refused to believe it was raining because he didn't have an umbrella!

I had a strange dream last night. It must have been a dream, otherwise I'm suffering from hallucinations, and that's not likely. (In the interests of objectivity—God save the mark —I'll put it down but, left to my own devices, I'd be tempted to do some expurgating.) I dreamed that I awoke to find an old man praying at my bedside. He was kneeling at the foot of my bed and it seemed that he was praying for me. It made me angry and I wanted him to go away, but he would not. I dreamed again that I was in a church, not a recognizable one, and that I was kneeling at the altar rail receiving Holy Communion. The wishful thinking motivated by witnessing the Christmas Eve service had pursued me into the morning. I awoke trembling and sick at heart. Ever since the dream, however, I have not been so disturbed. It was as though, for reasons beyond my comprehension, I had promised myself something—or was promised something—that would make the long wait easier.

January 10, 1956

It wasn't so long after all. The next Sunday, during the service, I realized, quite simply, that I loved God. There should have been trumpets and palisades rising into the air, bathed in a blinding supernatural light—but there were not. There was just a deep, quiet, sure recognition of a relationship that bound me, and arising from the recognition a love of Him that surpasses reason or imagination. I am still in doubt and division; I still do not qualify for membership in the Church; I do not even know His Name as yet. But love is a powerful lever. It releases in me a realization that now, not only is anything possible, but it is probable.

I can now see my way clear to enter the Episcopal Church's next confirmation class. So let the chips fall where they may. I will soon know what it's possible for me to believe. At any rate, I'm no longer running away. I am far from the faith of which you spoke so eloquently, but I do feel as if I'm entering into an experience that is very particular and very real.

II

Letter to Sara

Atlanta, Georgia
May 15, 1956

Dear Sara:

I am so glad that Kay introduced us! Friendships are so curious: sometimes you will be acquainted with a person for years without moving into a closer relationship with him, while with another there is an immediate yielding, a giving, a saying "yes" in so many areas at once that you feel you have known that person forever.

You and I have so much in common. First I discovered that we had both been through therapy—and with the same therapist—which makes us sisters indeed! Next I find we both have a daughter in the same nursery school. Now it turns out that you are a member of the same Church, and a convert at that. But what especially draws me to you is our similarity of response: you, too, are deeply involved and yet you, too, once had my doubts, my questions.

I cannot believe that in less than two weeks I will be confirmed! Rather, the rest of the class will be—as for myself, I have grave doubts. Our instruction period is drawing to a close; and, although I have learned a great deal about the history of the Church, the Sacraments, the Prayer Book, Christian doctrine, liturgy and ceremonial, prayer—I am even more confused than I was at the beginning. It's as though

I'd been studying the habits, culture, and beliefs of a remote tribe of peoples, remote both in time and in place. It
doesn't seem possible that such an anthropological survey
has anything to do with me. I stand very much amid the
alien corn.

If this is what Christianity is all about, it's going to take
a heap of doing to make myself a part of it. I even wonder
about the wisdom of such an undertaking. Is this really what
I want? It seems so at variance with what I thought I wanted
for myself. Please let me tell you about it. I must confide my
doubts to someone soon. We've discussed some of them, I
know, but I held back the full measure of my skepticism out
of respect for your faith. Yet you've said enough to me to
lead me to think you are one of the few people with whom
I can be completely frank.

I can't put all of this to my priest, Mr. Wood. It would
seem poor repayment for all his time and patience with me.
Besides, he doesn't take me seriously. He acts as if my doubts
were the most natural thing in the world and that I shouldn't
be the least bit concerned about them, that they will all come
out in the wash. Such blithe optimism is not the least bit
reassuring to me. He's standing on his vantage point rather
unfairly, it seems to me: after all, he's already in the fold,
of the elect, and one of those with the advantage of having
been "brought up in the Church." Since you, too, are a convert you are in a position to realize that it isn't quite that
simple. How can I, in the midst of my uncertainties, make
the vows that are required? I read through the Order of
Confirmation the other night, and I must say it did nothing
for my self-confidence!

I think it was when you asked me to go with you to the
Good Friday service that I first realized how ill-prepared I

was to embrace the faith. Since January I had been buoyed up with that "first fine careless rapture" which is the first fruit of conversion. It was enough that I had found God,* that He was drawing me ever more closely into a personal relationship with Him. In the divine-human encounter there is simply no room for doubt; it is a state of joy that one would not dream of questioning. But apparently it doesn't last, or the relationship changes, and I begin to wonder if I didn't imagine it all, or if it was born of my own intense need and desire. Furthermore, when faced with the necessity of decision and choice, the actual voicing of convictions—as in confirmation—becomes another matter altogether. A springtime romance is one thing, but marriage is quite another. It requires more than emotional response; it requires belief, trust, promises of perpetual fidelity, unconditional involvement, and a willingness to change the direction and content of one's entire life.

Why is it that when one who is seeking expresses any hesitation, let alone outright doubt, to a Christian, there follows a most embarrassing pause? It is almost as if one had spoken a dirty word or confessed to an ugly sin. There is an aura of unhealthy silence around disbelief, and it makes me wary. It makes me suspect that people are so unsure of their own faith that they will not risk examining another's doubt, which only reinforces my own suspicion that believers are all subject to an enormous delusion that can survive only in a climate of rigid dogmatism. Their answers, when they come, are hardly satisfying: "Well, you just know . . . " or, "You know it in your heart . . . " or, "The Church says so . . . " or, "The Bible says so."

---

* Rather, I now see, that He had found me. Beginners always think that they are taking the initiative.

I know I'm being unfair here: such questions are a threat to any but the most secure faith; I myself do not want to voice my own reservations. It is unnerving and humiliating to admit that I may have been deceiving myself or, if I haven't, that I am such an ingrate as to count the teeth of the gift horse. But the habits of a lifetime cannot be overthrown so easily. Therapy has taught me to observe and examine the unconscious influence of my own fears and desires, and the disciplines of philosophy require that I question all presuppositions. Moreover, if habits of clarification and validation are good practices in other areas of experience I see no reason to abandon them here. I keep hearing that there is no basic enmity between science and religion, that truth always bears up well under examination. Then let us see.

I think I've told you that I was unable to prove the existence of God on logical grounds—to my own satisfaction, at least. Since then I claim to have experienced God in some way, felt His presence, become aware of the beginnings of a person-to-person relationship. All this has so startled and delighted me that I have during these months been content merely to enjoy the experience quite uncritically. But, faced with the enormity of the step I am about to take in commitment to such a Person and such a way of life, I am roused into asking certain questions. I ask, since my reason has proved so ineffectual, how can my emotions be trusted? Might not all of this be explained on the basis of desire? There is no doubt that I *want* to believe in God. Man's need to achieve happiness and guard against pain can best be fulfilled or rationalized on the basis of a moral order in the world and life everlasting. But this cannot be accomplished apart from a Deity. Truly, our helplessness in a vast, deteriorating, and uncaring universe is made more tolerable by believing it to be animated by a concerned Spirit.

Isn't it possible that we win such comfort through the projection of our own personality upon the universe, and proceed to fabricate from within the evidences of presumed "revelation"? Yes, it's possible, especially among primitive and superstitious people. But is it probable among people who are well educated, honest, and essentially sound? Are education, honesty, and the health of body and mind any guarantee against self-delusion? They certainly ought to be. Can so many people be deluded? Well, they are every day, as P. T. Barnum discovered to his profit. Daily, countless people are hoodwinked, suckered, conned, and cheated out of, or into, all kinds of persuasions, largely on the grounds of what they want to believe.

Well, leaving others aside for the moment, what about you and me? You say that the timelessness and the repetitiveness of our experience of God wins over doubt. That makes good sense. In the field of science, if an experiment succeeds only once or twice its validity is open to question, but if it is endlessly repeatable with the same results, it commands respect. However, using the same analogy, suppose we have repeated our experiment to the point where we can be reasonably sure of our results, and all the while we are assuming that ingredient A is responsible for the outcome, whereas all the while ingredient B is the one which is the active factor. However valid the results may be, if the cause is unknown we cannot be assured of very much. Similarly, we don't need to know how or why such joy comes to us, but unless we know it comes from God we will not have a religion.

For example, I have observed that instances of unmitigated

delight occur more frequently during the period of the month from menstruation to ovulation. I know enough about physiology to know that the female organism is more responsive, more easily stimulated, more outgoing and yearning at that time than during the second stage of the cycle, which is more given to orneriness and depression. I realize that this is not conclusive in any way, but it raises a question. As long as we can associate any phenomenon with a physical or a psychological occurrence there is always the temptation to confine it within that framework.

Let's go back to the psychological for a moment. I say that I must be imagining all that has been happening to me, that I whomped it up out of my own need to believe in God. But has such a thing ever happened before? Have I ever been able to believe very long in the existence of anything that did not assuredly exist? This is an important question. If I had a history of self-deception I would have very good grounds for suspicion now. I can remember as a child how I longed to believe in elves, fairies, leprechauns, Santa Claus, but could never quite bring it off. Sometimes I would pretend to, in order to tease a playmate or please my parents; and I can remember lying at night in the middle of a little glen up in Vermont, straining my ears and eyes and all my senses to see the ghosts that I was assured by a reliable friend were there. The scene was certainly animated—by crickets, frogs, cicadas, owls, and the torpid breathing earth—but not by anything else that I could perceive. Children don't believe half the things their parents think they do. For poets and children the line between the "is" and the "as if" is clearly drawn, and they are never taken in by their own creative devices. Reality has a clear call.

Yet I cannot deny that my life has been touched of late

by something other-than-I. Can I confidently say that this "otherness" is divine, or is it simply an unknowable, indeterminate residue of myself? I must admit the whole Christian story is unlikely enough to be true. It's certainly nothing that mortal man would devise: it's too much against his own nature. We would much rather have omnipotence in the form of magic, self-glorification, and justification here and now, more like what the Jews had in mind for their Messiah. But Christ—what an unlovely, harsh, inconceivable Person! His very origin requires faith. His ministry makes sense only because we've become better oriented to His teachings, but in His time on earth it must have seemed like outright madness. And His death is the most incredible part of the whole tale—not that He should be crucified, but that He should choose to be, that it should be God's will that He die for something that men didn't even know they needed. At first glance the whole thing is utterly repugnant to me.

What troubles me most about the whole doctrine of salvation and Christian ethics can best be expressed by a recent entry in my Journal:

> Tonight I have good reason to be angry. I have social license to boil, to be outrageously and righteously indignant, to want to club my opponent in a gloriously primitive act of mayhem. The sad thing about all this lovely turmoil is that I can't feel or do any of these things. Before therapy I repressed not only acts of violence, but the anger which might have bred them. I was scarcely aware of being angry. Since then my emotional paralysis has been released, and with it the anger, whose expression on occasion I permit. I have been for a brief time the mistress of myself, custodian of many doors which I joyfully discover can be unlocked. Now that I am exposed to Christian ethics I am again asked to

inhibit various emotions and impulses. I am asked to check all my natural drives at their source and call upon God, not to help me, but to succor my offender, and I am invited to look to the life hereafter for vindication. This seems to me both unhealthy and childish.

It seems unhealthy because constant repression, whatever the reason, has morbid consequences. I realize that the religious person restrains himself, not out of fear, but out of obedience. Still, don't the same psychological injuries result? A colorless nonentity, devoid of verve and vigor? How can natural man be constantly checked without crippling himself? Doesn't the mortification of a turn-the-other-cheek discipline breed a kind of deadly passivity? No, it certainly doesn't sound desirable. Is it even good? When we think in terms of reward and punishment don't we turn the whole concept of salvation into a merit system? Isn't there, after all, in the idea of Judgment a good deal of our repressed hostilities seeking vindication? Milton Wood tells me that in the Greek the word "salvation" means "health of body and mind." It seems to me to be just the opposite.

And what about the continual searching of the conscience —doesn't it lead to a neurotic introspection, an egotistical preoccupation with self? For a religion that puts so much stress on the other fellow it seems like an inordinate amount of self-interest. On the other hand, the humanist concept of the dignity of man has far more appeal and, I think, realism. How can we love others until we first love ourselves, until we see ourselves invested with honor and stature as human beings?

I think that the Christian notion of "sin" is downright unwholesome. What is the difference between feelings of guilt and the consciousness of sin? Aren't they equally disabling in their effect upon the individual? During Lent we are exhorted to have "contrite hearts." Translated from the Latin this means "crushed" or "pulverized" hearts. *Why,* for heaven's sake? Isn't it more meet and right to "lift up our hearts" in the presence of God? But no, in our confession we are bade to "bewail our manifold sins and wickedness," we are "miserable offenders" who find our "burden . . . intolerable." This strikes me as utterly medieval. Because our remote ancestors used crude tools it does not follow that we do not have the right to enjoy the advances of technology. Or have we not progressed beyond the stinted and baneful precepts of Victorianism in our spiritual life? Is this "perfect freedom"? It sounds more like slavery to me. Is the cringing creature bent on appeasing his Creator's wrath the very same being who is made in His image? One would never know it.

All these paradoxical questions! I no sooner learn that one thing is true than I discover that just the opposite claim is made. Perhaps that is the chief attraction of Christianity: a person can be and have and do that which is mutually exclusive. All at the same time he can be both saint and sinner, fully free and fully dependent, both saved and doomed, immortal and mortal, God's chief delight and a creature incapable of pleasing his Lord! We can, apparently, live in a world which God never penetrates because He will not intercept our free will and, at the same time, we must reckon with a God who dwells everywhere in His creation and actively participates in the lives of His creatures. A dubious logic. No wonder Christians are so slippery: I no sooner have them pegged on one side than they pop up on the other side!

But what I find particularly objectionable is that I should be called upon to sacrifice precisely what I have been struggling to attain: selfhood. By that I don't mean selfishness. Although, to be honest, I don't want altogether to stop being selfish, I'll have to admit that many benefits could be enjoyed by myself and others if I were to become less selfish and less self-centered. (You see, right off I've made a mistake.

I'm not supposed to be thinking of all this in terms of personal gain. The setting aside of self is to be done for love of God!) However, I'm not referring so much to selfishness, although I can see that I'm going to have difficulties with it; no, I'm thinking about the matter of self-identification.

Until therapy I never knew for sure who I was. At a party, for example, I would behave with an aggressive person in one way and with a shy, retiring person in quite another way. I was like a chameleon, adapting myself agreeably to every person with whom I came in contact, altering myself to fit, to please; lacking a solid core of self. Consequently, I did not know what I believed, what I felt, what I was really like. Now, at long last, a personality is beginning to emerge. It's exciting to observe the emergence, to get acquainted with this person who is I, to see that she has certain tastes, idiosyncrasies, even emotions which are not based upon sanction but which arise from within herself. The thought of relinquishing that self before it is even known to me is disturbing. I hardly know what I'm to give up, and I certainly don't know what I'm to get in return. (There, again, I suppose I err grievously in that I'm not supposed to expect anything in return. But, come now, you don't seriously expect me to believe that Christians receive no recompense for their efforts! To say that virtue is its own reward is nonsense. The most virtuous people I know are obviously quite miserable.)

I think the matter of humility worries me most. Unfortunately I associate humility with a Uriah-Heepishness, an unctuous servility that is actually loathsome. Even I know this is not what is meant by "humility" in the Christian frame of reference. The best I can come up with is "meekness," but Mr. Wood says no, that's not it. He gave me a definition that didn't sound at all like humility—something

about reverence for others and teachability. I think he's trying to sugar-coat the pill. No, I'm afraid that humility is just
what the dictionary says it is: "Having or expressing a sense
of inferiority, dependence, or unworthiness . . . lowly in condition or manner . . . submissive, deferential." Frankly, I see
very little to recommend any of that. Having just conquered
such feelings, does it make sense that I should throw myself
back into such a mess?

Piety, I'm beginning to think, can be dispensed with. If I
thought for a moment that I'd ever be prey to the sort of
sentimentalized righteousness that is conjured up in my mind
by the word "piety," I'd run far and fast. I'm enormously relieved by reading a little book by J. B. Phillips, *Your God Is
Too Small*, which Mr. Wood gave me. Apparently he, too,
finds the "Bosom-Flyers" a mawkish lot, or those who conceive of God as—among other things—the "Resident Police-
man," the "Managing Director," or the "Grand Old Man."[1]
Fortunately, the sort of thing I find most objectionable is
found largely in an evangelical tradition and among elderly
ladies. Since I'm being so snide, I'll bet some of my outpourings sound about as languishing to you, but I must say you
put up with it all surprisingly well. You, dear Sara, seem to
have avoided the obsequiousness of humility, the paucity of
selflessness, and the pretentiousness of piety. Come to think
of it, I've not found much of that among those whom I really
know to be professed Christians. I'm encouraged to find
that both our priests, Milton Wood and Robert Mill, have a
delightful sense of humor, so my servitude need not be quite
so lugubrious as I had supposed.

You see, I'm still thinking of it as a kind of thralldom, a
perpetual bondage. Well, isn't it rather? Once I'm confirmed
will I ever again be able to call my soul my own? I must con-

47

fess that I've always resented being influenced by anyone in any ultimate way. Only love gives the right. Even then, in the most intimate relationship of marriage, there is an area of the self that is inviolate. I think even with men and women who are deeply in love, much as they might wish to relinquish everything to each other, they find it impossible. But now, after the briefest contact with God, I see that a full surrender will not only be possible but necessary. This is the point at which I am most uncertain. So it all goes back again to the loss of self. That is my Jordan.

Much as I need reassurance, I've found that the people who have the most profound effect upon me confront me with the truth. A physician once told me that I was a coward, and since then I have been able to be much more resolute and relaxed. More recently Dean de Ovies, whom I consulted at the Cathedral of St. Philip on a matter not at all connected with religion (or so I had supposed), said something that really knocked me back on my heels. He told me, as closely as I can remember, "You have a very vital and overpowering ego. Turned outward toward God, you will go far, but turned inward, as it is, it will destroy you." No amount of rationalization could convince me that he had not spoken the exact truth.

Oh, Sara, how can I admit now that I thought I was all right as I was, that I didn't need or want to undergo any further change! Yet I did need to change, and I still do. A seed of doubt has taken root, and it grows steadily and strives against the hard-packed soil that must have lain over my mind all these years. When a man begins to suspect that he may not be his own reason for being, it is a terrible moment.

At any rate, all this seems to give the lie to my earlier contention that religion merely satisfies what we desire, that it is so much wishful thinking. Here I am hesitating on the very opposite grounds! It's true that I don't want to relinquish my self-assertion, my self-identification, my self-sufficiency, yet that is precisely what is being asked of me. By whom? The Church? Couldn't I simply become confirmed and proceed to participate in all the outward forms without experiencing any inward change? There is no doubt that this is done every day, but could I do it? I suppose I could, yet what would be the point of it? It would be like cheating at solitaire—no real gain. Besides, I don't want just the Church, that's secondary. I want God. Is it He who requires the sacrifice of my selfhood? Apparently so.

But hold on a minute—before I become enamored all over again. You and I have both read enough of the lives of the saints to realize something more. Aren't the people who are notably religious certain "types"? I don't mean that they are fanatics or disturbed people—not at all (at least not all!)—but simply that they seem to exhibit certain traits that might predispose them to seek satisfaction by means of a Deity. Aren't they imaginative people who contrive make-believe domains and people them with heroes and villains and even some ordinary persons, and display remarkable inventiveness in the structure of government and society? To use a modern example, C. S. Lewis did that as a boy in his "Animal Land" (*Surprised by Joy*).[2] How easily this type of projective planning might be expanded into the Kingdom of God and all life hereafter!

Aren't these people receptive to, and hence more readily subject to, the hypnotic persuasion of any evangelism? And haven't truth and beauty been equated for so long that even the most loutish would hardly dare deny the connection? One can scarcely be a lover of nature without being a lover of God.

Aren't such people, almost to a man, idealists? What could be more natural for those who are frustrated in their search for the perfect to find the Perfect? For those who are disappointed in reality to find indemnification in Reality? Aren't they essentially impractical, unfitted for competitive life, socially inept, sexually immature? Aren't they offered in God precisely what they lack in man—compensation, refuge, a surrogate of sorts? When I was in college the unwanted, the girls who never had dates, became "grinds" or else they turned to religion, sometimes both. The bride of Christ—she, too, can be ravished. And where else do we find the cause of weaklings better championed?

From here we move into the pathological. And don't we find among the insane the same delusions? Those who imagine they are immaculately conceived, those who speak with "tongues," those who are magically immune to that to which the rest of us are liable . . . or those who must suffer, who expiate their guilt through flagellation. What is the difference between the masochist and the martyr? How do we distinguish between the paranoid who believes he is persecuted by an unseen enemy and the person who believes he is tormented of the Devil? Wherein lies the difference between the man who suffers hallucinations and the man who claims the vision of God? If all the demands of sense and reason fail, doesn't the mystic take refuge in the "ineffable"?

Of course, none of this is any kind of proof that God does not exist; it may indicate just the opposite—that such characteristics in people best render them susceptible to God's influence. But to deny that such attributes are characteristic of religious people is foolishness. I, myself, have a number of these traits. I, myself, claim to have found other-than-myself, to have experienced God in some ineffable way. So what is my first impulse? Why, to assert His existence, of course. How else could I defend my ego against the charge of abnormality and delusion?

I think, really, that this must be the answer. Man desperately needs the extraordinary to lift him out of himself, to attach importance to an otherwise drab life, to make tolerable the intolerable, to explain the inexplicable. He cannot simply invent God because his reason would soon find him out. So his unconscious mind fabricates a transcendent experience, not wholly emotive—again, because his reason (if it were at all trained and alert) would make short work of such nonsense— but an experience that places demands on the total self, perhaps not completely credible, but certainly compelling, such that it cannot be dismissed on sensory or rational grounds. It cannot be that we simply "fantasy" God. No novelist believes in his own characters. He creates them and may even forget them, but he never deceives himself that they have any reality apart from his own creative imagination.

Here I become dubious of my own argument. This must indeed be a rare function of the unconscious mind, that all other avenues of escape should have been apprehended, other secrets revealed, and this—the capacity of the unconscious to create God—remain undetected. You would think that someone, sometime, during man's long history, would have caught himself at it. The atheist denies God, but he does not say, "I've found myself out, caught in the very act of compounding the deity who is, I now see, made of so many parts defective reason, so many parts distorted sense data, so many parts will-to-believe."

All error, all delusion is sooner or later—no matter how hurtfully—corrected, revised, denounced. It requires only one honest man with the courage to admit he was wrong. We once thought that the sun revolved around the earth, but Copernicus demonstrated that quite the contrary was true. It was always supposed that light must travel in a straight line until Einstein showed that light bends when approaching a gravitational mass. But who will challenge, with proof, the existence of God?

So, what am I left with? I have discovered that the religious experience, while it may embody many of the characteristics which I find suspect in other areas of experience, is more than these. Gordon W. Allport claims that "the psychological roots of religion have nothing to do with the validity of religious experience."[3] He explains that the ways in which people conceive of God—however pathological those ways may be—do not invalidate their experience of Him. We are deceived when we class this experience by its roots and not by its flower, its fruit. I suppose we always think we have exhausted the question when we try to dispose of God on one level. Furthermore, we simply don't expect Him to operate through natural means. What could be more disarming than that God should come to us through His own creation! Yet we always expect Him to operate above and beyond that.

I have discovered that I have a not unreasonable preference for that method of inquiry which can function through the senses. If what is to be known cannot be measured, I am bereft. It is quite natural. We should not expect to determine the weight of an object or the number of degrees in the angle of a triangle through prayer. It's possible, without doing violence to our reason, that spiritual realities can be apprehended only spiritually.

It seems to me that confirmation is not so much a time of commitment as it is a time of preparation, not so much a finishing of faith as a germination of it, not an end for a

Christian, but the means by which he becomes fully one. If discipleship is primarily an invasion of the Living Spirit, then Mr. Wood is right, and I am asking too much of myself. I need only prepare myself for His visitation; I need only voice a willingness to believe and to obey.

If I were capable of total belief and full obedience I would not be ready for confirmation—I would be ready for heaven! If preparedness for entry into the Church lies only in saying "yes" to God, then I must be confirmed. For who among us can be overshadowed by the Almighty in any way and be capable of anything else? We may protest our capture, and struggle for release; to save face we may argue pro and con and try to convince ourselves that this was our considered decision. But when all is said and done, do those of us whose lives have been touched by God ever have really any choice afterwards?

I cannot now know exactly where I stand on points of doctrine. My surrender is to theism, not to Christianity, but that seems to me at this point irrelevant. I know only that the pull is too strong to resist. We do not need to understand the law of gravity in order to be obedient to it.

I reason this way: if God exists, then whatever my confirmation vows entail will be required of me, whether I like it or not, whether or not such fealty is what I thought I wanted for myself. All such questions become comical. I have no option but to follow Him, to learn His will and to be obedient to it. If, after my confirmation, I should discover adequate grounds for believing that God does not exist, I can in all conscience ignore my vows—since they would then be meaningless—and commiserate with myself upon having been taken in by such an incredibly clever hoax—rather like Pascal's "Wager."

In the meantime I want only to relinquish myself to the overpowering pull which draws me closer to what I both fear and desire with all my heart. You, too, have experienced this awesome attraction, this incredible joy. Some day perhaps I shall be able to share Good Friday with you. Right now it simply overwhelms me, and I don't know what it means; I know only what it signifies. For its meaning I will have to wait. Perhaps when I may partake of the Sacrament of Holy Communion I will be closer to an understanding of such a sacrifice.

I hope I haven't shocked you by any of my hairy heresies. It's done me a world of good. I don't feel nearly so confused as I did. I dare say it would be surprising if I did not experience some rebellious uprising before the day of reckoning. But if I go as a lamb to the slaughter, I go as an uncommonly sportive creature. Now that I've laid my doubts aside it is probably just as well that I am ignorant of what lies ahead of me. I refuse to visualize a dark and straitened way beset by thorns. It seems as if God Himself were shining on my path. I am reminded of a passage from *Meditation For a Young Boy Confirmed:*

> This kneeling, this singing, this reading from ancient books,
> This acknowledgment that the burden is intolerable, this promise of amendment,
> This humble access, this putting out of the hands,
> This taking of the bread and wine, this return to your place not glancing about you,
> This solemn acceptance and the thousand sins that will follow it, this thousand sins and the repenting of them,
> This dedication and this apostasy, this apostasy and this restoration,
> This thousand restorations and this thousand apostasies,

Take and accept them all, be not affronted nor dismayed by
    them.
They are a net of holes to capture essence, a shell to house
    the thunder of an ocean,
A discipline of petty acts to catch Creation, a rune of words
    to hold One Living Word,
A Ladder built by men of sticks and stones, whereby they hope
    to reach to heaven.[4]

III

Letter to Milton

Atlanta, Georgia
August 6, 1956

Dear Milton:

There is something I should like to tell you before I leave Atlanta and, since words come to me more easily on paper and since there is so much to say, I have decided to write you a letter.

The other day after I talked with you and made some parting with my past, I realized I had moved into an entirely new relationship with God. It is so different that I am tempted to repudiate what went before. One is always inclined to see growth in terms of audacious leaps and ignore the small agonizing in-between efforts; actually, in one capable of growth, I suppose there is a continual unseen movement beneath the surface.

During the whole of the Communion service yesterday I was in the grip of such a terrible struggle, besieged by so many conflicting doubts, that I felt like running headlong from the church. I could not understand what was happening to me. Now I do—at least more than I did then.

Last summer I was engaged in a similar combat: I was trying to extricate myself from my therapist as a father-figure and establish my own independence. These last few weeks

56

during your vacation I have, without realizing it, been trying to break free of you and establish a relationship with God that is independent of you as an intermediary.

One of the hardest things about leaving therapy was that I had to go out into the world and assume responsibility for my own growth. So it was that I had, without recognizing it, not only come to God in a large measure through you but had continued to nourish and sustain that relationship through you—being too fearful of the personal responsibilities of entering into such a relationship on my own.

With the thought of leaving for Nevada (now that my husband has accepted a position at the University there), I was suddenly faced with the loss of what small gains I had made toward becoming a Christian. Despite what is generally supposed, I don't think one automatically becomes a Christian when one enters the Church. Supposing, I reasoned, my parish priest there were not so mature, so knowledgeable, so understanding as you—then I would surely lose what I had so painfully gained. And, although I know it's foolish, I cannot convince myself that I will be able to find God in Nevada!

I did not foresee the struggle I suddenly became involved in yesterday. Just as before I had had to make the choice between remaining a little girl in relation to life and blundering forth into adulthood, so I must now make some advance toward God. I am far from serene about the choice I made yesterday and I am sure there will be a good deal of blundering, but I feel that now, at long last, I have cut myself free of my utter dependence upon you—or anyone else—and can now reach God myself. Don't misunderstand me: I do not believe that any kind of growth can be accomplished all by oneself. I shall need people, perhaps even more, to help me broaden and deepen my relationship with God, but my belief and love of God are no longer dependent upon others.

It's clear to me now why I felt somewhat guilty about taking Communion, becoming confirmed. I felt I had no right to these Sacraments. In a sense, I didn't because I was a Christian in name only; but they did serve their purpose in helping me to become one.

It is a fearful thing to face our Lord. It is a terrible thing to fall into the hands of the Living God. I haven't been ready to lose my life so that I might gain it. I suspect it is because I have not yet been prepared to accept insecurity, to abandon myself to an even greater risk so that I might be able to achieve a sound relationship with God. I was too concerned with the salvaging of my ego, with my timorous anxieties, with the job of vouchsafing for myself and for my family the various gains and securities I felt we so desperately needed—all the while withholding from them the fullness of my love, even as I withheld myself from God. Even as I denied it, I kept insisting upon a division between the temporal and the eternal man, the ordinary and the extraordinary.

Gradually I have come to see that I must accept man as a total being, the spirit commingled with the mind and with the body, God's involvement in my daily life and with that the necessity of my involvement, to the largest extent that I am able, in the fullness of God. This requires the assumption of a rather frightening responsibility, the total reckoning of myself, the willingness to possess for myself salvation or, as you call it, health, to put off from myself the avenues of escape I have been using.

I never intended it to mean this much. I don't believe I imagined I would be required to be or do or become or even to believe this much—until I was ready, and then I could always pull out if it got to be more than I could handle. It is difficult to be a Christian; it takes more courage than I ever dreamed to loose my anxious hold on the things about me and abandon myself to God's absolute governance. But I have learned this: the reason I could not experience God's mercy is that I am only now beginning to recognize my own personal sense of sin. Now I can see the difference between that feeling and the twisted, immature, guilt-ridden feelings of my past. With a sense of guilt one is passively remorseful, permeated by a despondent hopelessness; but with a sense of sin there can be an active repentance, and one is permitted to be restored to God without being destroyed. This is a far healthier state of affairs.

I do still experience a good deal of confusion in my convictions. I do not see eye to eye with the Church on many matters! I cannot understand how we can so cheerfully accept the hypotheses of science, the concept of millions of solar systems, of an expanding and infinite universe, and at the same time cling to childish and anthropomorphic conceptions of God. That not only puts a limitation upon man's insight and growth, but it presumes to limit God. I do not believe, for example, we can have any "pictures" of God or of our existence after death, except those we clearly recognize to be of our own making. I believe, as I think you do, that the Bible is a record of man's struggle to find God and God's reaching down to man, and as such reveals man's capacities and his incapacities. I am coming to see that man can have a knowledge of God so long as he does not insist that it be hatched in the shell of his own brain.

When I was a child I pictured Christ as a friendly fisherman, a benign shepherd, a sort of super father-figure. I could not then realize, or conceive of, the agony or compassion of

His manhood reckoning with the terrible mortality of man, of His crucifixion or our redemption—nor can I even now, but I'm beginning to have glimpses of it. Just as my earlier conception of Christ has grown, so do I expect my present one to grow. I see no reason to put limitations on it. I think my confusions will be resolved as I come to know God better.

All I can say now is that I accept the basic doctrine of the Church, but I am convinced that what I believe is a product of my culture, my training, and the accident of my birth. I cannot presume to limit truth by rejecting the possibility that it may not be confined solely to the Christian religion. There are a number of other matters about which I am still in doubt —the existence of the Devil and of angels, the concept of purgatory, the intercession of the saints. My Protestant mind has still some hesitation about various ceremonials and rituals. But when I look back to the utter confusion of last year in which I blindly approached God, without belief and without love, I am astonished I could have come so far. I find again and again that whenever I take a decisive action in regard to God, as I did yesterday, I am unbelievably filled. I pray that I can continue to make those strides, and now that I am faced with the necessity of breaking free of the props, it may be possible to achieve some real growth.

There is one thing that gives no promise of being resolved, and I hope to be able to talk to you about it before I leave. I seem to be tending more toward the attitude, the feelings, the experiences of the mystic. I am coming to see and feel and know God as ineffable and real.

I have always felt—and still do for that matter—that the experience of the mystic is essentially unhealthy and unsound, and is activated by some basic incapacity. Yet I am faced with a dilemma in myself: the closer I get to a relationship with

God, the closer I am drawn into a vigorous and realistic relationship with my husband, my family, and friends and acquaintances.

Still, the urgent, wondrous, and unbelievable fact is that I have made a start. Before, I was testing my strength, getting ready to get ready, but now I have broken the ground and the structure has begun—the structure of a relationship I will be building all my life, with thanksgiving.

As I knelt yesterday, tears came, and I remembered that I had not wept at leaving my friends in Ann Arbor or in New Haven. I had been too rigid, too fearful of involving myself that deeply in other human beings. I had never really loved people, so I could never really suffer at the loss of them. Now I was involving myself in a relationship with God that would be even more demanding, but I was confident that I need never lose Him because, for the first time, my relationship to Him was not dependent upon any one time or place or person.

My debt to you in all this is very large. I thought all I could return to you was gratitude, but now I think I can do more. I can soon do for others what you have done for me— not so expertly, not so knowledgeably, but I've acquired enough now to start giving as well as taking.*

This letter has been delayed because, even before I finished it, I was inundated in a dozen different matters—finishing off my interviewing job, acting as liaison officer in the sale of the lot and our furniture, and starting the long task of sorting and packing. It's going to be quite something to get off by the end of the month.

---

* It was to be three full years before I was ready to be of any real help to others. It was evident that God was not willing to put me to use until my desire to help others proceeded, not so much out of my own need, as out of theirs.

Apart from anything else, I still have reservations about our new life in Reno, Nevada. Reservations? Ha! I'm just plain scared. I can't think of a more improbable place to take up residence. I enjoyed living in Ann Arbor; New Haven had variety and excitement; Atlanta has given me not only the Church but many friends and much beauty. Reno, apart from the no doubt exaggerated connotations about gambling and the divorce mills, sounds high, dry, and barren. I had so hoped to make our home in Atlanta that the move away fills me with a great deal of sadness, and I find myself resisting it. Women are so curious: once they acquire children and land and start putting down roots, they, who once craved the unknown, variety, and change, become reactionary and stubborn!

My best to you, and please say goodbye to Anne for me if I do not see her again. I thank God for you and for All Saints' Church. Please remember me in your prayers, as I will you and a number of the other wonderful people there.

I still wish I could have been nourished a few more months in my "Mother" Church. I wonder if God knows what He's doing in pushing me out of the nest so soon!

IV

Letter to Madaline

Reno, Nevada
March 30, 1957

Dear Madaline:

When you asked me last night how we were liking Reno,
I was really ashamed of myself for making such a ruckus
about the move! We love our new home and, while I agree
with you that it's more difficult to get acquainted here than
in the South, the climate and the mountains make up for so
much. All the overwhelming scenery, dotted with deep for-
ests, rivers, lakes, and snow-summited mountains, catches my
breath in my throat.

I had had qualms about my religious life here, too. I was
foolishly concerned with outward forms and with personalities—what the new priest would be like, the appearance of
the church, and so on. It was a radical change for me. Nothing
could be more different from the mysterious, subdued, elaborate grace of All Saints' Church than the rough, elementary,
forceful interior of Trinity Church, all bathed in a blinding
desert light. Here there is no hiding place, no distracting
murmur of traffic, only an empty mountain silence. There are
fewer creature comforts. Not here can I rest my haunches on
the seat when kneeling! Not here can I become lost in a mul-
titude of people. Not here do I find sanctuary. It is more like
an ambush. It is an uncompromising grandeur in which I am

63

isolated, in which my senses can no longer wander off into a warm labyrinth of beautiful detail. I feel stripped and naked in the presence of such a combative and penetrating power, a power that borrows something from the vastness of the desert and the loftiness of the Sierras.

I wonder if this austerity is to set the keynote for my religious life here! At any rate I'm glad we are meeting more people like you and your husband. We so enjoyed having you both for dinner last night and, while a phone call would suffice to tell you this, the subject of our conversation about the nature of God started me thinking.

In the light of my reactions to this part of the country, it is easy to see how the awesomeness and majesty of God at work in His creation is singled out as almost the hallmark of divinity. But if we stop here, as you have, we are able to see only a God who is infinitely powerful, infinitely perfect, and infinitely angry. If we see Him only as a Judge, don't we forget that He is also all-loving and all-provident?

I think it is man's nature to be stunned by the immensity and complexity of the universe. From his beginnings man has stood in awe of infinity and experienced a numinous dread that the void might be personed by the supernatural. To many of the early Hebrews "Yahweh" was a fearsome God to be reckoned with through propitiation. Today many of us fear God, particularly in our beginnings. We know that as a baby develops in the womb he recreates at every stage the racial development of man. So it is in every expansive phase of life. After we take our first tentative step toward God and until we reach a union with Him, our growth in a sense recapitulates man's historical religious development. We begin haltingly with doubt and intimidation, and as we grow we achieve assurance and love.

All of us have experienced the numbing effect of generalities upon the imagination. We are curiously indifferent to the staggering enumeration of thousands of men killed on a battlefield, but let one man die whom we knew and loved and the heart is wrenched from the breast. You asked me how we could love a God so vast, so impersonal, so indifferent to our destiny. I said I didn't think we could, and you were puzzled by my reply, so I'm going to try to clear it up. No, I don't think we *could* love such a God, and that is why I feel that the people of the Old Testament were limited in their capacity to love, not only by their own restrictions, but by the limitation of God's revelation.

"God so loved the world that He gave His only-begotten Son"—here we are given something that we can experience and understand. I believe that Christ came not only for our redemption, but also to make of the Infinite a particular One, to make the Divine human. The Son of both man and God was capable of hunger and thirst, sorrow, suffering, and temptation; He came to move among us and form a bridge of His Body and His Heart across which we might falteringly make our way to God. That is universal love made particular.

That is all very well, but, you ask, what if one cannot believe in the divinity of Christ, in the Sacraments, in the Bible, in God Himself? At one time Christianity was a closed circle to me. It seemed, at first, as if one step were contingent upon the next, as though one must accept that next step if he were to accept the first, and so on. There was no place where one could break in to get a toe hold. My very presence in church, I reasoned, was hypocritical since I couldn't believe anything. I was armed only with a desire to believe, if it were possible, without violating myself. Everyone does it differently. Some people can be honest enough with themselves so that it is not necessary for them to rationalize their need—they can come to God in the midst of their failure and bring with them only their insufficiency, and for them the Kingdom of God is closer at hand than it was for me. I was a dozen steps away from anything that simple! If you back up into skepticism and agnosticism about as far as you can go, short of atheism, that is where I stood.

If you are capable of overcoming that I-don't-belong-in-church-because-I-can't-believe rationalization, you can always find æsthetic pleasure in the liturgy itself. Here I had an advantage not only in the dignity and beauty of the Episcopal services, based on the venerable language of the Prayer Book, but in my parish, in All Saints' Church, Atlanta, I found charm and grace and spaciousness. I was a willing foil to its deep-throated organ and magnificent choir. It was not surprising, for I have always been impressed by beautiful churches and always enjoyed sacred music—the glorious Masses of Beethoven, Mozart, and Bach, to name but a few of my favorites. To me the creative works that Christianity has propagated were a cherished part of man's heritage. With Santayana I lamented that it was so beautiful it was a pity it wasn't true!

I was fortunate at least in this: because of my background I did not have to overcome the deeply rooted prejudice against the Church that you are struggling with. I sometimes think it is better to have no religious background at all than to have one which disables us. Wasn't it St. Augustine who compared this state of affairs with the man who, having had a poor doctor, was afraid to trust a good one?[1] There are many who are in the same dilemma: they feel endlessly culpable in relation to God and are consequently always hampered and insecure. They cannot forgive themselves, so they cannot imagine that God can. In this I feel that some Protestant denominations are at fault: to have engendered in so many such a distorted view of Christ's teaching, to have planted in the fertile ground of man's weakness such a sense of guilt on the one hand, and on the other a concept of such an indifferent, unrelenting, and even vengeful God that it is small wonder that the house of God should have become distasteful to many and to not a few an unconscious reminder of their own overwhelming impotence. In my opinion, this is the offense of fundamentalism.

Since my own incapacity to love fully had been removed during therapy, my love was at last free to flow toward God, unimpeded by the crippling restrictions of a deformed conception of Him. And it was then that I finally broke through what seemed to be a closed circle, and found myself in the untenable position of coming to love a God in whom I did not believe! Recently I mentioned this to a friend, herself a Christian, and she only smiled knowingly and said, "Oh yes," as if this were the most reasonable thing in the world. To me it was unnerving, and I was sure that I was engaged in the worst sort of self-deception.

I suppose there are as many ways of coming to God as there are people. This was my way; and even today I could not prove the existence of God on rational grounds. The inability to demonstrate Him as one would a geometric theorem troubled me. I reasoned, and I feel properly so, that the doctrines of the Church were axiomatic: that once you assumed the first of them as "given," then, of course, all the rest would follow—at least logically.

But how does man go from his first step of belief to the Infinite? I don't know. I don't think we can know. We are as incapable of grasping God as we are of fully understanding a seed in a flower pod. We are equally ignorant of the microcosm and of the macrocosm. "Since he [man] is infinitely removed from comprehending the extremes, the end of things and their beginning are hopelessly hidden from him in an impenetrable secret; he is equally incapable of seeing the Nothing from which he was made, and the Infinite in which he is swallowed up."[2]

However, belief is fortunately not dependent on comprehension. None of us can be content with a small portion of faith; we find that it is a surprisingly stimulating nourishment. There comes the time, for most of us, when we are ready to take the leap of faith; it is a wonderful moment, ringed round with as much truth as any of us can hope to know. I don't think it's possible to drift along indefinitely without taking a stand. It's what the lawyers refer to as a "live option." God does not act upon us against our will, but it is amazing how far He will take us if we are ready to take even a small step. Incredible? Yes. It is past the understanding of any of us, ever. Yet unfailingly it has happened over and over again.

When I was a child we used to play a game called "Giant Steps" in which each player was allowed one step forward—a baby step (one foot's length), a scissor step (a jump with feet spread apart and then together), a giant step (a long standing broad jump), and so on. The object of the game was to reach the goal first and, although each had his turn, the "monitor," who decided what kind of step we should take and so determined our rate of progress, always seemed arbitrary to me and to indulge at times in favoritism. I imagine that's the way God seems to many of us. But whether we move ahead one foot at a time or take that long flying leap forward, we will be proceeding as fast as we are able, that is, as long as we do not miss our turn.

This helps me to learn how to take a laissez-faire policy

toward Bob's spiritual life. At first it seemed incredible to me that he could not understand my convictions or my growing wonder and delight; I was puzzled and hurt when I realized he could not share any of it with me. Whenever he attacked my faith, as he did frequently, I became alarmed or angry. I had not yet acquired enough knowledge to defend my growing convictions on a rational level, and it was utterly frustrating to try to explain my relationship to God in terms of experience because it was still obscure and ineffable. The blindness that had once been mine appalled me when I met it in another. How embarrassed I am at my earlier criticism of the defensiveness of Christians—here am I, in my bullet-proof vest, cowering on the back porch!

I am still betwixt and between. Even now I cannot accept a few beliefs of the Church, for, in spite of my impatience in other ways, I move slowly and cautiously. It's the only way I can do it. What I can lay claim to I have made mine through experience, reason, and faith. Someone once said that what you cannot comprehend in relation to the Creed, the Bible, morality—whatever—should be left alone, for sooner or later it will become clear to you. That is greater wisdom than I am presently capable of attaining. Yet it has been so for me. Had anyone told me that some day I would in time be able to believe, let alone have any insight into, the Incarnation, the Trinity, the Sacraments, the Crucifixion, or the Resurrection—to name but a few—I would have been too alarmed to proceed. It is not without reason that God fills our cup of faith only to the measure it can contain. But like ourselves, it can grow —and that, as far as I can see, is why we are here.

It is hard to find a place to begin, but if we had to start with the Infiniteness of God I do not think most of us would have the courage to begin at all. So begin where you can, perhaps in small, daily things, in homely ways, remembering that Christ walked them, too—but begin.

I am a fine one to be giving advice—I haven't got that far! It would be better had I started here, in the small homely ways. Now I have to go back to the Primer. It reminds me of how dismayed I was in college when I discovered that, in order to study astronomy, I, who had never had much math, was compelled to know something about logarithms. Because of my deficiencies I didn't get very far in that subject. Logarithms are rather prosaic but they do help unlock many of the secrets of the heavens.

We certainly have enjoyed seeing you in the Little Theatre and hope your work in the plays won't keep you and Philip from dropping in on us again soon.

V

Letter to Bishop Lewis

Reno, Nevada
July 1, 1957

Dear Bishop Lewis:

You are out of town for the summer, and I've been back from our trip over a week now. I think I mentioned that while Bob was teaching a brief summer school course in Las Vegas the children and I visited my family in California. Since I do not know if I will be able to get an appointment, I've decided to write to you.

A curious, disarming, and frightening thing has happened: my faith, my love, my total relationship with God have been disturbed in some way, sometime since I left Reno and, possibly, after I returned. I have been trying to understand it and am completely at a loss. I cannot think of any one act of mine or any one event that might have brought such a thing about. My only conclusion is that my faith must have been very weak to begin with, and my love surely misplaced—yet that is incomprehensible. My faith seemed to me illimitable, and it was an orderliness by which my world turned on its axis. Now everything seems to have changed inexplicably.

I think I may have first sensed it before I left home. Perhaps I was already slipping away, but I now put it down to the busy-ness of leaving—ends to be tied off, packing to be done, the house to be put in order for our return. I next noticed it the first Sunday away from home. The parish church of my parents is not unfamiliar; even if it were, could I not carry God with me? Had it something to do with my family? No, it was surely the nicest visit we have ever had. The old disharmonies have long since been dissolved. The occasional impatience I experienced there did not constitute a barrier between myself and them, so how could it between myself and God? Was it some latent, inhibited evil that sprang up, that my conscious mind modestly halted? I really don't think so, for therapy has enabled me to be cautious in such matters.

It must have been a "barren period," I reasoned, all the weeks I was away. But they don't last that long, they never do—a few days at the most.* When I returned I realized I was faced with something far more serious than spiritual impotence. It seemed as if I were catapulted back into all my earlier doubts. The deep, fulfilling joy, the sustaining belief, the being a part of other human beings, the desire to help others, the constant, unfailing cycle of receiving and giving, giving and receiving—all were interrupted.

I began to believe, in my anxiety, that Trinity Church here had a talisman of some sort, as had All Saints' in Atlanta. Surely when I returned and was able to worship here again, the difficulty would be routed and the old order restored. When it was not, I grew even more alarmed. It was as though my faith had been an illusion, as if it had never existed at all. The practices I had followed, even Church services, although familiar, could not be reckoned with; so little of me responded, so much of me worked in blind directions—

---

* This astonishes me now! Since then I have gone as long as five months without any conscious contact with God. I never cease to protest it, but I have learned that the longer the "dry" period without God—especially if it can be borne with equanimity—the deeper, for reasons that I cannot yet understand, are the spiritual rewards.

part desperately trying to ferret out the why and wherefore, part looking on sardonically, rejecting God, and a small part asking to be restored.

About this time our three-year-old son contracted a particularly stubborn virus. He had never before been really ill, and, tired from the long trip home, I had to tend him night and day. The constant loss of sleep which both of us endured did not help any, and I became increasingly irritable with him. I, who am capable of such tenderness with my own children! I was astonished at my shortness in every way.

Just afterwards, an acquaintance of ours, an elderly, patrician Frenchman whom I shall call Adrien, came to Reno to gamble. He often invited us to come with him, and twice I joined the party and played the small amount we could afford to lose. The first evening he lost nearly $3,000, and I was very upset over his loss, although he didn't seem to mind. Gambling is one thing that could never become a vice with me —I'd become too anxious over it. It's all very well to say it's only money, and while money is no longer such a desperate thing with us, to some people it is, and as long as it is, losses make me anxious. But that should be no concern of mine.

What all this has to do with my separation from God I do not know, but it seems to have at least something to do with it. Oh no, it is not the morality of gambling. I don't think I have any strong feelings on that matter—unless it would be a question of temperance, but that applies in other areas, too.* Yet I did notice one thing: an overwhelming

---

* Later I came to have some reservations about gambling. Even when not abused, when considered solely from the point of view of entertainment, I sometimes wonder if it does not foster an attitude of getting something for nothing. With some people it can become a disease, as destructive as alcoholism or narcotics addiction.

avarice—something I've never been aware of before, certainly not to this extent. My husband won't agree with me, but I feel that we live comfortably. Occasionally I get a yen for a new hat, or I'm disappointed that we can't invite the So-and-so's over because we can't afford to entertain as often as we should like—but usually I manage quite happily to keep my desires within the framework of reality. Yet here I was, unexpectedly and ridiculously, frustrated and greedy on a preposterous scale. I was jealous because a bachelor who never had to worry about money in his life could afford to lose in a few days what my husband earns in a year; I was envious because I thought he could, instead, contribute that sum to some worthy charity—namely, us.

But what does this have to do with my decline and fall? I know only that soon, less than two weeks after my return, I began to lose my confidence. The old feeling that I-might-as-well-be-hanged-for-a-goat-as-a-sheep prevailed, and I behaved very goatishly indeed. (Just so no one can build a morality tale out of this, let me add that I won $22 during Adrien's stay!) I began behaving nefariously with people, I neglected my work, I spent less time with the children, and my relationship with my husband worsened. Again I was afraid. . . .

I don't know why I put this in the past tense; as far as I know, it's still going on, but it's easier to write about it this way. Over and over again I ask myself, how do I know my faith in God wasn't an illusion? Could something I wanted so much that I made it come true by my own will and my own need, be similar, in any way, to the miraculous cure of an hysterical illness? I can't say. Certainly I was changed significantly, as were my relations with all those around me; having once experienced faith, I could never deny that I was happier and more whole than I had ever been before. But, I ask myself, cannot a man's need and will accomplish this—if it is strong enough? If you use belief as a bridge, will it not, though unfounded, lead you across an abyss? If a man believes his parachute has opened, will he not, at least until he lands, experience less fear than the man clawing at the air?

So, how do things stand? What was it that separated me from God? I thought surely that it must have been one appalling thing, but now as I write I see that it could have been many smaller things. There was busy-ness, for one thing; my life was too cluttered those last hectic days to cultivate God's friendship. When we returned to our "garden," we were dismayed to find everything overrun with weeds and much too dry; after all, we'd paid a rather indifferent fellow to tend it. Then, I suppose I did not really believe that God would be in California any more than I believed He would be in Nevada after I'd left Georgia. Could it have been an unconscious desire not to please my parents too much, a bit of adolescent show of spirit? Since this was what they've always wanted for me, why should I oblige them? Added to that was my being demoralized by fatigue and concern over my son, by avarice, jealousy, and from there neglect of myself and others, and by a fear that breeds faster than rabbits.

Is this the continuity of separation—the small attrition of events wearing away the structure? But, I protest, *that* takes years! This has happened all within a month. Was my faith, then, so unsubstantial? What can occur under the stress of a real crisis if this is what can happen after a few snaggings? It seemed formidable. Am I living still in illusion? That I still have a small portion of faith, that I still believe—is this, too, a deception? Can anything be trusted that gives way so readily? I feel absurd, cheated, and, at the same time, stricken.

Again, how will I ever be able to grow in relation to God

if I proceed on the ludicrous assumption that He is only among the familiar, the best beloved, the secure, the knowable? All of this speaks of uncertainty in me. Like the turtle whose shell is his protection, his home, and his very life, I must learn somehow to carry God with me. I thought I had. I dare say that is why so much emphasis is put upon the authority of the Church—to avoid this kind of impasse.

I am assuming I can return to, or reach ahead to, the point where I can again call God my own, dwell in Him and He in me, but I have good reason to be frightened that I can't. Anyone who has ever known God will understand how I feel —it is like giving up your life within life. It is easier, I suppose, to relinquish your hold on things when disaster is inevitable, but to me none of this is so inexorable that it cannot be changed. It must be changed. It's impossible to go back to what I first was in relation to God, not caring; my difficulties from now on are going to be the result of caring too much. What happens then? I become angry with myself for my witlessness and take it out on others or, less likely, hurt so much I apathetically retire into myself. Either prospect is chilling.

One thing is certain: things cannot stand as they are. I have this characteristic: I cannot for long be at odds with a person, even when I make serious mistakes in breaking the deadlock. I used to think this was impulsive; now I know it is compulsive. Milton Wood will tell you this has something to do with my impatience. But how do we grow without impatience? How can we bear even a partial loss of God? I cannot bide my time. I cannot even pray.

Perhaps you can tell me what to do. At any rate it's warming and helpful to put it on paper, and I do thank you for listening.

Do you know, I almost feel as if I were mending already, as if I were dissolving back into myself in a gentle relinquishment. Ah, how good it is to start to feel whole again, how appalling to be scattered and divided. It seemed, for a while, as if the old monkey were on my back again—that saw no evil, heard no evil, spake no evil—the blameless one, untouched by life and apart from all humankind; that permitted me to be blind and inflexible; that permitted me to love with only a part of myself, the other part looking on with the sardonic amusement that corrupts love; that permitted me to beseech God for reinstatement without integrity. Yet how can one in decision command the rest of oneself in division? How can one be reconciled again to the whole? What have I done to permit this recommencement of the healing process? Or what has God done? Has the overt act of sitting down and facing it through words made God's grace available to me again? But whatever and however, I take it to my heart with thanksgiving.

July 6, 1957

There have been a few occasions since my children were born when one of them suddenly and inexplicably developed an alarmingly high fever only for it to have dropped by the time we reached the doctor. I cannot help thinking with irritation that the child might have stayed sick at least until we reached the doctor's office. I am similarly embarrassed now that I have finally secured an appointment with you, and wonder if I have any right to appear when my problem is almost resolved.

I have been reading Monica Baldwin's delightful book, *I Leap Over the Wall*, and have discovered that the siege I have been under is far from being isolated, that it is quite common in religious experience. She calls it "spiritual desolation" and says:

> As a rule, one is first attracted to prayer by the joy and sweetness that one finds in it. (People who never pray will obviously think that this is nonsense. Well, they are mistaken. It is a fact that there is no happiness on earth which can be compared to the happiness that is to be found in prayer. How, indeed, should it be otherwise if prayer is what the saints declare it to be—conscious contact with a Being whose very nature is Love?) And the first months or even years in the Noviceship are often spent in a state which is the spiritual equivalent for being in love. As a result, nothing is hard; one is carried along by a kind of romantic enthusiasm which makes of Religious Life an earthly paradise.
>
> And then—often suddenly and for no apparent reason— the sunshine vanishes. Instead of the warmth and colour that have hitherto permeated everything, a dreadful depressing greyness—a dyspepsia of the soul—blights every detail of one's life like a bleak east wind. The almost rapturous sense of God's love and of His presence which made of each hard thing simply an opportunity to prove one's love, gives place to a feeling of terrifying solitude in which one becomes dismally aware only of the stark realities of life. The entire spiritual world seems meaningless and unreal; even one's own most vivid spiritual experiences fade out like half-forgotten dreams. . . . Bitterest of all, one is beset by horrible temptations to see in Religious Life the most fantastic of all delusions and oneself as a pathetic fool for having undertaken it.[1]

What disturbed me most in the whole matter was my inability to pray. When one is cut off from God, one has only the bleakest kind of faith to fall back upon—and I'm afraid mine was not of much comfort. Yet I remember that no matter how dismal things became—and they did become quite stark—there was never any question of turning back, of thinking I might just give the whole thing up as a bad job. Do you remember that last February I told you I had already reached the point of no return? However daunting my condition may be there is nothing to be done about it except to try to change matters as soon as possible. The withdrawal pains are far too unnerving to be endured for very long. I simply don't believe that St. Teresa put up with such a condition for over twenty years!* Or if she did, I can't think of any excuse for it.

It's been suggested by various people who should know, that all of this is a form of discipline by God. I hope those who hold this view will forgive me my brashness in saying that I think this is pure nonsense.† I believe that we, and we alone, bring about such estrangements, abetted by the co-operative nature of evil—the Devil, if you prefer. No wise parent ever threatens a child with the loss of his love; he will discipline him in other ways—he will remove even good things from him if by so doing the child will learn better—but he will never withhold himself, otherwise the very foundations of their relationship would be destroyed. Didn't Christ say that if a human parent knows how to give good things to his children, how much more our Heavenly Father? If we cannot believe this, how can we accept so much of the Gospel that

---

* Having later read St. Teresa's *Life*, I discovered this was not true. There was a period during which she could not pray, but this lasted somewhat less than a year. The twenty-year period she speaks of refers to that time during which she was perfecting herself in the service of God and, while it fell short of the kind of devotion she came to expect of herself, it certainly did not constitute a separation from God.

† I had somewhat to change my mind about this, too! See Letter to Hugh, p. 110.

repeatedly claims that God is always, unfailingly, and continually there for those who ask and knock and seek?*

People are always counselling me to patience, and I am sure they are right most of the time. But when it comes to setting right a disturbed relationship with God I think it should be done with alacrity. Isn't that precisely what a child does when he has alienated himself from his parents? If his relationship to his parents is proper and healthy, if it has not become warped or repressed, the child himself, without any action on the parents' part, will become so desolate and miserable that he cannot rest until things have been patched up. To delay merely makes everything more difficult—as anyone knows who has ever tried to "make up" after even a small, long-past misunderstanding with a friend.

For those of us who have known God, He is the stuff out of which we grow, the raw material with which we lessen the breaches, anchor the destructive elements, recreate daily the positive rudiments in our lives. So to be without Him, even for a short period, is at best tenuous, at worst perilous; and I see no reason whatever for prolonging it. There was one perceptive nun who, according to Miss Baldwin's report, claimed that we must at times "wrest" from God what we must absolutely have.[2] It reminded me of Jacob wrestling with the angel, and I can easily understand with what agony he at last cried out, "I will not let thee go, except thou bless me!"†[3]

---

* Later in my reading I discovered some support for this conviction in St. Francis de Sales when he writes in his *Spiritual Letters* that Jesus alone was forsaken of His Father, when He hung on the Cross. His nature alone could endure the withdrawal of the Father's presence. St. Francis concludes that if God were to deprive us of all else, He would never deny us Himself as long as we desired Him.

† But I must add that we should be careful to distinguish what we think we so desperately want from what we absolutely must have; they are very

You might ask how I did manage at last to set things right. To me, at the present time, there is no "tried and true" method. I have to experiment. Perhaps later I can work out a technique if this sort of thing happens again, and it seems that it will. In this case I phoned two friends, Father George and Father Ned, and their assurances both as to God's availability and, even more reassuring for some reason, as to their own availability, were a solace. I am sure that each must have been comfortably in bed at the time, for it was quite late when I came to the conclusion that I simply could not spend another hour in such division. It is a heartening thing to be able to talk to someone who believes as you do. I remember once in Atlanta, long before I became a member of the Church, I phoned Robert Mill, who was then curate at All Saints', for similar assurance. At that time I was making a rather futile effort to believe in God, and despite everything that I myself tried to do, I could not quite bring it off. Bob Mill made what seemed to me a remarkable suggestion: he said I should simply say, "God, I cannot believe in You tonight," and go on from there. I was rather dubious about just where I could go from there; but the suggestion that I might bring anything to God —even my disbelief—was encouraging. From then on I felt a considerable affection for God, largely because He would put up with such nonsense in good grace. (Lord Elton once remarked that, although it couldn't be very flattering to God to be chosen chiefly as an alternative to hell, it does show forth the abundance of His love for us![4])

It was still some time before I began to be capable of

often not the same thing. Perhaps God Himself is the only "all" that we absolutely must have. At any rate, no one can "use" God, it simply cannot be done. I've tried it. I suspect many people have, but I've never known anyone to succeed.

any real love for Him, but it was a start. Someone once said that God is very patient with beginners, and perhaps that is why, once we get started, everything goes so well at first. If we had to deal with God in any mature manner at the beginning, I don't believe we should get very far. That may be why so many of us go so very little of the way toward a full relationship with Him. As the going gets harder, when we reach an area where some real growth is expected of us, it's so much easier to stand still. We forget what Jesus meant by comparing the Kingdom of Heaven and a little child: He did not mean that we should remain in a static childishness.

What He pointed to, primarily, was simplicity and humility. Now, neither of those virtues has been noticeable in me; they have been for me what is known, I believe, as a stumbling block. Perhaps the brief and almost casual telephone conversation with the two priests was a humbling experience in itself. At any rate, the gratitude I felt for their unreserved help enabled me, even with abortive prayer, to go to sleep with an assurance that all would be well.

The next day I took from the day's activities two uninterrupted hours for myself. Anne Lindbergh tells in her book, *Gift from the Sea*,[5] how necessary it is for women, especially those upon whom others depend, to vouchsafe for themselves routinely some time of solitude in which they can "fill up," after being drained by a life of activity and fragmentation. It is an excellent idea, but, as she recognizes, it is quite another thing to achieve. However, for women who are responsible for a home and children and a relationship to their husbands they want to maintain, let alone deepen, it is necessary to have some time alone. So with Mrs. Lindbergh's advice in mind, and the advantages of the single-minded contemplation Miss Baldwin speaks of, and the friendly encouragement of Father George and Father Ned, I went to my room. (I once asked Milton Wood how he thought God revealed Himself and he said mainly through people, through books—not exclusively the Bible—and through the Sacraments. I think we too often forget the first.)

What happened after I closed the door to my room is going to be difficult to describe. I know only that for the first time in nearly a month a channel of prayer was opened to me and I was able to make my confession without any obstacle. From then on the natural and fulfilling needs of prayer were met, to my wondering astonishment. Encouraged, I plunged on. I, to whom fifteen minutes of prayer is sometimes arduous, found unrestrained joy in nearly an hour of it.

This led to an amazing thing: I found myself filled with that simplicity and humility which I had not yet experienced. To experience God in even a small way is a humbling thing, but to be rewarded with such largesse of His rich mercy was staggering. I fell at once into that creature capacity I had known of but was not yet willing to make mine, and experienced for the first time an overwhelming worship and adoration of Him. I had not known how to do this before. I had loved God, I had respected Him, I had tried to keep His commandments, but I had never truly and joyfully worshipped and magnified Him because I had never before had a true sense of my own position in relation to Him.

I had felt the lack of it in me before. The great hymns of praise, the canticles of rejoicing, the Psalms especially, art, poetry, the Masses in music form—man's outstanding efforts to reproduce his sense of illuminating smallness in relation to God's unspeakable Self—I appreciated them first æsthetically and later, when I was able, with human insight, but never before had I felt active participation in them. There had been indications, from time to time, that this might be possible for me; but it was something beyond my understanding, and so I dismissed it from my thoughts. I wanted to involve myself in it, and yet I did not want to appear queer if I did. But the reality of God is pervasive and stabilizing. In the back of my mind all the time had been the misgiving that mysticism was definitely a sometime sort of thing, but once I'd crawled out of the hole of my psychological inadequacies it seemed a shame to throw myself back into it on religious grounds.

Now, someone is bound to ask me if this isn't all a substitution for sex. I honestly don't think so, for the very reason that the farther I go in relation to God the more capable I am of being a mature woman. However, there is no doubt that God uses our sexuality, as He uses all aspects of our nature, and consecrates it to His service.

All this brings to mind the repeated and natural inclination to think of union with God as being equivalent to the union between a man and a woman; and I do think it's a very good simile. It is not the same, of course, and yet it is the only thing that a man or a woman has to use for a comparison. As sexual union lifts one out of oneself into an area where desire and love are identical, so infinitely more does the love of God lift one indescribably out of oneself into a mystical union with Him.

In that moment when my adoration of God exceeded anything I had known, I asked humbly that I might know God more fully. I had never asked before; I had never been in a position to ask before . . . I may never again. And gradually, as if something luminous had been uncovered, I experienced God—in that white heat of Him, moving from the inward need to the outward reality, lifted up unto the periphery of Christ. The blinding colors, the light, and the warmth were merely sensory efforts to record a profound experience of the heart.

How can I tell you of it! It is as if our loneliness is cupped within the void, brimming to the rim of possibility. Nerve quickens, the soul is unshielded . . . tensed, chest-aching, spirit-glad . . . to burst the mortal shell and dance in pæans of rejoicing, archway after arch down a vistaed aisle! This is the pivot of articulation, wordless but understood. This is the threshold of living: we stand upon an Olympian crest while something very akin to pain leaps through us, and joy rolls out like thunder.

I might have stayed there longer, but I simply could not bear it, it filled me to overflowing. Now I understood with sudden clarity why people sometimes try to do away with a sense of self (which I thought was a very good thing) and impose self-denying and self-limiting (which I thought was merely a martyr complex*). Now I can better see the need to hollow out ourselves so that we may the more contain God.

Thus I turned away from Absolute Love, from the phenomenal fulfillment of myself in God, because I was not yet capable of receiving Him. I did so not regretfully nor hurtfully, but expediently and with the knowledge that I might return. Therein lies the miracle of man's relationship with God—the "still again." How incredible is His mercy that He would permit, in the very midst of my doubt and division, an access to Him that I thought surely belonged only to the saints!

---

* This term has been greatly misused. I use it here in the popular and psychological sense. While it is inaccurate, it will at least be understood.

July 11, 1957

Although I have since talked with you, I'd like to add a postscript to this letter. You made me see, as no one else has, how faith must become independent of emotion, and how emotion cannot be made a trustworthy guide to one's relationship with God. His presence or absence cannot be determined by one's feelings. You mentioned the case of Father Schleuter who told you how, having become separated from God, he discovered the importance of continuing—doggedly if necessary, and without the slightest emotional reward—in one's habitual contacts with God. How do you know, you asked me, that what I was able to establish through prayer during my period of blight was not effective? Indeed, how could that overwhelming experience have been given to me otherwise?

I had been thinking of it quite differently. I had felt that my emotions were a reliable guide to God's accessibility to me —perhaps even to "proof" of His existence—and that is why my faith was so disturbed. I felt that it was futile to approach Him in the midst of my doubt and deprivation—that I was being hypocritical. I even felt dubious about continuing in intercessory prayer, as if its effectiveness devolved upon one's accessibility to God, as if those not "in grace" had no right to appeal for others. That, I now see clearly, makes the whole thing man-centered rather than God-centered.

While I was able to see that God's existence was not dependent on me, I was not yet able to see, until I talked with you, that God's dwelling in me and I in Him did not depend on how I felt about it. Knowing this may not make my next loss of contact with Him any less uncomfortable, but it certainly will not allow the unseating of faith that happened this time. Formerly it seemed to me that the position you take was much too rationalistic; I see now that reason and will provide a safeguard that cannot be found in emotion. Miss Baldwin said it made her hackles rise to be told that a ten-minute prayer in desolation was worth a hundred times that in consolation.⁶ I can see how a prayer offered up in the midst of one's barrenness might be cold comfort, but it does not necessarily have to be unproductive. I don't believe I've got quite that far yet! It reminds me of St. Paul's adjuration to be babes in belief; it's plain that I, being unskillful, am still using milk —which is as it should be, I suppose—but I would be lying if I said I weren't impatient for the "strong meat."⁷

Today we put a good deal of emphasis not only on emotion, but on an effortless, full-blown-from-the-head-of-Jove sort of thing. If you have to work at a relationship it loses half its charm. The way so many young women of my generation were prepared for marriage (myself included) is a good example of it. Almost totally unprepared for a healthy sexual life, and woefully ignorant of household tasks and money values, we judge our relationship to our husbands primarily on emotional grounds. While we are still overcome by sentimental feelings we are capable of acts of charity and tolerance, but once this kinship threatens to move on to a more adult level, marital jaundice sets in. So it is only when we change the working "picture" of ourselves in connection with others that a more mature relationship becomes possible.

This is what you meant, then, when you said one need not remain a child in relation to God. Even though I've known that it was true, at least theoretically, it's thrilling to be rid of the shackles of one's infantile dependencies and move on to the freedom of claiming that image of oneself which is like unto God.

I am grateful, not only for your having taken the time to

talk with me, but also for having interested me in attending Camp Galilee at Lake Tahoe during "family week." If we could possibly manage it, it would kill a number of birds with one stone. The children have needed the vacation our trip south could not provide: unhurried play and contact with other children. I have long needed a chance to discuss religious matters with other people on a supervised basis. Christianity, by its very nature, must be communicated. The whole program there sounds ideal and I do hope we can come.

VI

Letter to Sister Veronica

Reno, Nevada
September 28, 1957

My dear Sister Veronica,

An aunt of mine, a writer and an inveterate correspondent, always used to say that the person who went away wrote first. So I have waited expectantly for your first letter; but now that a month has gone by with no word from you, I have decided to reverse the convention.

If only we could have had a little more time, one or two more meetings! I hated to see you go and at the end was fighting back tears. It's surprising to me that I could have made a friend of you in such a short time; I have many acquaintances, but friendship is something that usually requires a long period of nurture. Let me tell you how very grateful I am to know that it had meant as much to you.

By now you will be quite settled in your school routine. How does it go? Are you finding teaching such young ones rewarding? I should think that they would be hard to handle if you've never done it before. And how do you find the community at Stockton? Do let me know all about it.

Shortly after you left, our little chapel, St. John's at Lake Tahoe, was consecrated. What an impressive ceremony it was! I can't remember ever seeing our Bishop quite so ceremonial, decked out in his cope and mitre, with more than a dozen priests in attendance. Father Wes, who led the discussion group at Camp Galilee, celebrated—and, oh, how beautifully. I once told him that if he had not entered the priesthood he could always have been a ballet dancer, he moves with such admirable ease.

You see my penchant! At times I'm a little ashamed of my love of the æsthetic in form and ceremonial; it is true that our Lord is no less present in the rudest little chapel and in the simplest service, but I cannot help being moved by the fullest kind of glorification of God as, for example, in the *Missa Solemnis* of Christmas Eve.

After the service I had an opportunity to visit with the Mother Superior of one of our communities in San Francisco, a teaching order. She and many others had come up to the camp, not only for the consecration ceremony, but for a week's retreat which was to follow.

Let's see—what have I been doing? My husband and I observed our fifteenth wedding anniversary by going out to dinner. We had planned to go somewhere to dance afterwards but met some friends at dinner and went back to their home, where we talked until four in the morning, and I discovered that the days are past when I can stay up half the night and manage children and household the next day!

There is something I wanted to say to you before you left that I did not have either the time or courage to say that last day. I wanted to tell you about the loneliness that one finds in the habit of dwelling in God, or desiring to, as I have done. By the very act of permitting God to be the purpose of my existence I seem to have set myself apart from my fellow man. So, I reasoned, there must be something amiss, because the very opposite should occur: I should be drawn, through loving God, into closer relationships with people, with my

family. There is no contradiction between the two parts of
the commandment. But to do this, to love God with all my
heart, soul, and mind and at the same time love my neighbor
as myself, I must enter more fully into the lives and activities
of others. It is not enough that my capacity to love is deep-
ened; I must also do something about it.

I had been becoming a bit discouraged and disheartened
lately. In my headlong search for God I seemed to have succeeded only in irritating my husband, puzzling my Bishop,
arousing the amused forbearance of my friends. For the most
part, my urgent need to talk to others about God went unsat-
isfied except when I came to the convent and talked with
you. I became convinced that my fervor was not only spiritually profitless but perhaps not what God intended for me. I told
myself that it was intolerably egotistical of me to presume that
God had given me any special grace above others whom I
knew and, since the others could not hear Him, who was I to
say that I could? I reasoned that my dwelling in God and He
in me should bring forth fruits of incalculable splendor—instead I had nothing to present but a rather ordinary life,
changed, of course, heightened and intensified, but still not
more holy or more virtuous; not crowded with good works;
not noticeably more compassionate or generous; not at all a
witness to God's overwhelming mercy and love. I told myself: go back to (or rather, on to, since I had never really
lived it) the life of a sober, self-contained Christian; learn
slowly and patiently the virtues of such a life before you dare
even call yourself a follower of Christ.

So, for the last month I have become involved with people, things, places, events. It was not at all difficult to do, for
the advent of autumn brings the beginning of school and the
familiar cycle of activities gets into gear again: faculty events,

Church programs, teas, P.T.A., the Little Theatre, outings, and social events. It's been pleasant to see more of people, for I had felt deserted during the summer when everyone seemed to disappear or to be overcome with inertia. I love the fall; it is my favorite season, a time when my blood stirs and my senses respond to the impact of so much color. Everything seems to change: the clouds are brighter, the shadows denser, the air more fragrant—with sage and leaf mold.

I have lived again during this month the kind of life I lived before I experienced God intimately. I led a full, reasonable, well-rounded life, discharging my duties, enjoying my leisure in reading (detective stories, articles, poetry, seldom religion), playing with the children, entertaining friends. God's name rarely crossed my lips, and it was a relief not to be looked upon as queer and suspect. I did not feel separated or alienated from God. I attended church and partook of the Sacraments as regularly as before, although not as joyfully. I maintained my relationship with God, a more casual one, through prayer that became dutiful and almost perfunctory. I was, on the whole, perhaps less tempted to sin and became almost satisfied with my conduct. Here I was living the life that most Christians do, and I was miserable.

So I have to look again at the "givens." I am as I am—as God has made me to be. It is false humility to question His many gifts to me, for as I acquaint myself with the lives of others who have sought Him out, I see that His giving cannot be a mark of honor based on merit. God alone knows the reason for it and I am only being ungrateful to question it. But, since I lack humility, do I really question it? I think rather that I am merely rationalizing because, first, I am not yet prepared to throw myself entirely on His mercy and give myself unreservedly into His hands; and, then, because I am cowardly and afraid that indeed it will be a harder, straighter path, that it will involve a great deal more of myself—what I want to give and what I do not want to give. And, yes, loneliness. But when it is one's chief joy, strength, aid, the very foundation of life itself—what else is there to do?

Was my relationship to my husband, children, friends really bettered last month? Not really; it was only more peaceful because certain controversial and questionable matters were, if not eliminated, at least tempered. And I was deprived of the deep, sustaining wave of happiness which God gives me in a closer relationship so that, while the irritating grains of sand which stimulate the growth of the pearl were removed, I was left with an empty shell. We cannot, I see, really have a relationship with God without being deeply involved, even when our involvement leads us into error. Our very mistakes in relation to God lead to growth—when we care enough.

I sound as if I were making a choice. Well, perhaps I am. Perhaps we have to choose anew every day between God and turning our faces to the wall to die. As God continually re-creates us, so we must continually recreate our relationship with Him, through Him. I suppose this is the meaning of growth. But I certainly will be glad when this awkward, in-between stage is over! It's a kind of spiritual adolescence in which one is extremely self-conscious about all one's experiences, altogether too introspective, and everything is a little too meaningful. One wishes to stop being such a trial to oneself and others, but it isn't a matter of will; one must simply live through it. Yet, from what I know of adolescence and adulthood, there is something in the earlier stage that we wish we would not outgrow entirely. If with spiritual maturity, in becoming an effective Christian, in learning how to take myself less seriously in relation to God, if I were also to lose that spontaneous delight, that being on tiptoe with expectation, I should regret it very much.

Take yesterday, for example—with what unspeakable gladness my voice responded in the familiar passages of the Communion service: the *Kyrie, Credo, Sursum Corda, Sanctus, Agnus Dei, Gloria in Excelsis!* What a tremendous difference there is between my meager participation of the last month and yesterday's full-hearted rejoicing. All my efforts toward religious sophistication collapsed. But do we really worship God otherwise?

There has been a change, though. Since the time of my brief union with God earlier this summer, I have not been afraid. Before, I was buffeted about by doubts and anxieties, but now there is a kind of serenity in me. The headlong drive to do everything at once, the impatience to be perfect, to bear fruit immediately, to please Him in everything, is lessened. Instead comes assurance, an acceptance of myself and of my dependence on God; however depressing my own unworthiness, I must not allow it to overwhelm me. I must take whatever I am, at any moment, to God. I must believe and act upon His promises declared unto mankind that He will, upon our true contrition, pardon and deliver us from all our sins, so that we may approach His altar and partake of His Body and Blood—even as we are. It is not before the Consecration in the Eucharist that we can meaningfully offer ourselves to God, but *now*—now that Christ has made up the difference. This is what I learned at Camp Galilee.

Now the continual round of sin-repentance-absolution has become less discouraging, and I know that, with God's help, I will be able to amend my life, to bear tangible fruit, and bring others to Him; I know also that I cannot accomplish it all overnight or in my own way—but in His time and at His will. So it's easier to remember to check my enthusiasm before those who would not understand and to wait more patiently for those, like yourself, who will.

Who am I to say this? Anyone who has experienced the reality of God, even for a moment, will know that there is something timeless about that moment; one can see oneself *sub specie aeternitatis,** and it becomes impossible to take oneself too seriously and God seriously enough. I look forward to another year of slow but sure growth. How many things I will have to learn, and how eager I am to learn them!

October 7, 1957

It's now a week later and I have been busy with my telephone interviews and have had no time to add to this. About all my free time has been taken up with reading St. Augustine's *Confessions* (I was so fascinated by it that Sister Mary Barbara gave me her copy!) and St. Teresa's *Life.*†

I am astonished at the insight St. Teresa reveals. (What a begrudging remark! But, you see, I have never read any of the lives of the saints until recently, and I had always shared the common misconception that they were remote, other-worldly escapists, that they must have been suffering from various psychological derangements that shaped and colored their response to God.) It's been such a pleasure to read her *Life,* and I keep exclaiming, "Oh yes, *yes!* Exactly. Quite so." Although I'm still not convinced that I am not suffering from delusions, it's comforting to know that another human being

---

* Literally, "under the aspect of eternity."—Ed.

† St. Teresa of Avila.

has experienced much the same thing with all the accompanying misgivings and reservations and, even more amazing—considering the differences in temperament, training, culture, profession, and separation by nearly four hundred years in time—that we should have reached almost identical conclusions! That is, I hasten to add, at our *beginnings*. She very quickly outstrips me: by the time she reaches the fourth level of prayer we have definitely parted company and I have to follow her not on the basis of personal experience, but through sympathetic insight alone.

I keep saying to myself, if only I had had this book during the summer, when I was so confused and was forming the conclusions I put down in the earlier part of this letter. On the other hand, it might not have helped; perhaps, after all, valid conclusions can be based only on the trial and error of one's own experience. But oh, how encouraging it is to know that one is not alone in that experience!

How I wish you were here to share these books with me. If you were, I am sure you would ask what especially impressed me, what particularly cheered me in reading, say, the life of St. Teresa. I remember your saying that you, too, had read her life not too long ago and that you asked me to give you my impressions when I could get around to it. I don't suppose we get quite the same thing out of it, for your needs are somewhat different from mine. As a beginner, I largely identify myself with the experiences of the saints in the areas of their failings; whenever they botch something, I can take heart, and when out of their confusion comes clarity and out of their failure comes success, I can rejoice with them.

I had had a sentimentalized, idealized conception of the saints: I had vaguely supposed that after a certain point they led serene lives of unruffled perfection, unstirred by any of the difficulties which beset us! (Or, if they did run amuck, they certainly wouldn't write about it.) I imagined that they were untroubled by rational reservations, that their faith was steady, that their progress toward God was as inevitable as if they were mounted on rails, that the grace with which they were endowed (due entirely to their holiness) was totally different from what we run-of-the-mill mortals knew. I wonder if many people have such a bizarre misconception of the saints? Why, with God's help, they are exactly what you —and even I—can aspire to become! Indeed, exactly what our Lord expects us to be!

For example, I spoke of my discontent with a small portion of God's grace, but St. Teresa says, disarmingly:

> It may well be that I am judging others by my wicked self, and that there may be some who need no more than the truths of the Faith to enable them to perform works of great perfection, whereas I, wretched woman, have need of everything.[1]

Father Juan d'Avila, to whom St. Teresa's manuscript was sent, gives his opinion thus:

> Nor should anyone cause alarm by condemning them forthwith [who have experienced God's grace], because he sees that the person to whom they are granted is not perfect, for it is nothing new that our Lord in His goodness makes wicked people just, yea, even grievous sinners, by giving them to taste most deeply of His sweetness. I have seen it so myself. Who will set bounds to the goodness of our Lord?—especially when these graces are given, not for merit, nor because one is stronger; on the contrary, they are given to one because he is weaker, as they do not make one more holy, they are not always given to the most holy.[2]

97

Given to us because we are weaker—this makes me limp with relief! I no longer have to bear the burden of pride, of responsibility, of all those foolish questions as to whether I have the right, and so forth. Christ came especially for people like me—"not to call the righteous."[3] It is the sinner who can repent who is in the enviable position. I can ask boldly for God's grace, His help, His healing, simply because I need it more than others. It is only the forgiven who can know how good God really is.

In regard to my ceasing to pray (during that period of separation from God), which I concluded was a rationalization based on mistaken humility, St. Teresa says:

> But it is necessary that we should realize what kind of humility this must be, for I believe the devil does a great deal of harm to those who practise prayer by encouraging misunderstandings about humility in them so as to prevent them from making much progress. He persuades us that it is pride which makes us have ambitious desires and want to imitate the saints and wish to be martyrs. Then he tells us, or induces us to believe, that we who are sinners may admire the deeds of the saints but must not copy them.[4]

Here is one of the reasons I came to seek you out:

> . . . But if a single person begins to devote himself to God, there are so many to speak ill of him that self-defence compels him to seek the companionship of others until he is strong enough not to be depressed by suffering. Unless he does this he will find himself in continual difficulties.[5]

Then, there is another passage which reminds me of the advice my Bishop gave me some time ago, a truth I have discovered for myself over and over again:

There is another temptation which is very common—namely to desire that everyone should be extremely spiritual when one is beginning to find what tranquility, and what profit, spirituality brings. It is not wrong to desire this but it may not be right to try to bring it about unless we do so with such discretion and dissimulation that we give no impression of wanting to teach others.[6]

She cautions against our allowing our sense of unworthiness to overwhelm us.[7] And she speaks of the mechanics of prayer: how we must forget about the organization of prayer in order to make any progress.[8] How apt that is! I remember in the beginning, when I was learning how to pray, I would remember the five parts of prayer: confession and forgiveness, petition, intercession, thanksgiving, and adoration. Later on it was necessary for me to rid my mind of all "helps"; otherwise, like the centipede who stops to consider which of his hundred feet he puts forward next, the movement of prayer would collapse altogether.

Then there is this amusing bit of advice: "In the early stages, then, one should strive to feel happy and free. There are some people who think that devotion will slip away from them if they relax a little."[9]

How exactly she describes the way God teaches us: "When His Majesty so wills He can teach everything in a moment, in a way that amazes me."[10] And how lavishly she describes the rewards of these experiences.

However, it was the *Confessions of St. Augustine* that particularly delighted me. I saw that St. Augustine, too, was a convert and struggled to make peace with the demands of his reason and his vision of God, to conciliate the claims of his selfhood with what God required of him. Here I also stand—

but not, I'm coming to see, alone. I'd like to set down the high points, taken from the *Confessions*, of what seems to me to be typical of the Christian journey, particularly for those of us who start with nothing and end with All. Here is a pilgrimage that bears the marks of what I feel is sooner or later characteristic of every Christian experience.

We start out with such similar questions, and so often come away from our inquiries empty-handed. "For the others whom I had met, when they failed to find answers to the questions of the sort I posed, promised me Faustus."[11] ". . . Of the sort I posed. . . ." How well I know—all those naive questions, those embarrassing questions, that will not leave us alone and cannot be given the *coup de grâce* through our most persistent explorations. We are always promised a Faustus, but he never quite succeeds in satisfying us.

There is only One who can do that. The greater our learning, the greater the obstacle of our first growth in God. Later, when we can submit our minds to God's instruction, it becomes an asset. "Surely a man is unhappy even if he knows all these things [philosophy, mathematics, astronomy] but does not know You. . . ."[12] Yes, but we are the happier for St. Augustine having known both!

"But where was I when I sought after Thee? Thou wert there before me, but I had gone away from myself and I could not even find myself, much less Thee."[13] This is the universal testimony of the seeker who must lose himself in the midst of his finding. We start with questions, seeking answers, and come to lose even a sense of what the questions are, let alone the answers, and must wander about in a cloud of doubt.

Wandering in that wasteland of skepticism we decide to set up hypothetical conclusions to guide us. How urgent it is for man to come to some conclusions about the nature of reality! He simply cannot exist in an empty room without manufacturing furnishings, even though they do nothing to comfort him. St. Augustine does not permit himself comforts for long, however; he is beginning to discover that our assumptions do make a difference, just as he found it does matter what we are happy about. Mere decisiveness, like mere happiness, cannot survive unless it is grounded in the truth.[14] The mind, in acquiring beliefs, must begin with a clean slate; skepticism to be fruitful must be open-ended.

What happens next? We can almost guess with what caution he will advance and with what despair he will retreat. But I doubt if we should all bear such sour disappointments so well; I, for one, protested loudly over what I felt were God's grudging revelations. St. Augustine hesitates over the problem of evil, he cannot come to grips with the infinity of God, he is troubled with our Lord's humanity—how can it be united with His divinity without debasing His divinity? He is torn between Catholic and heretical doctrines, between the aspirations of his spirit and the requirements of his flesh. He frets over what he may have to give up. He is encouraged by St. Ambrose to learn that "the letter killeth, but the spirit giveth life."[15]

Is not St. Augustine voicing our own experiences?

Furthermore, St. Augustine's greatest difficulty was my own: "I wanted to be as certain of things unseen as that seven and three make ten."[16] Thank God our reason is not the only means by which we can find Him! "Thus, since men had not the strength to discover the truth by pure reason and therefore we needed the authority of Holy Writ, I was coming to believe that You would certainly not have bestowed such eminent authority upon those Scriptures throughout the world, unless it had been Your will that by them men should believe in You and in them seek You."[17]

I am convinced that a person who is equipped only with determination and the Holy Bible has an excellent chance of finding his way alone—alone except for the hidden Spirit, instructing and guiding. (I am not claiming that we do not need the Church, for how, without the Sacraments, could we become grafted to Christ? But God is not so limited that He will not use many means to bring about our conversion.)

In what straits St. Augustine found himself! There he was in Milan without the help on which he had counted, eager for faith, but not knowing where or how to come by it. He says nothing about going to church. Perhaps he was hampered by his mother; she may never have actively proselytized him, but she never ceased to let him know that his conversion was her dearest and most determined desire. (We see where he gets his determination!) We certainly cannot blame St. Monnica, but how many of us, particularly those of us with a stubborn cast, have been put off by the zealousness of a well-intentioned relative?

There he was—up to his knees in heresies, with no help from books about the Church and its doctrines (such as we take for granted); the Bishop, St. Ambrose, was too busy to instruct him, and he had no Christian friends. Goaded by impatience and frustration, he asks, "But where shall I search? . . . And, in any event [if he were to read], where can I find the books?"[18] It must have been a real problem to such a scholar, but personally I think it was just as well he didn't find the books he thought he needed; they might have served merely to confuse him further. Thus, he was forced to find the message of the Gospel directly, through the only Christian book he had.

Eventually he finds Christian friends, and from one of them he hears about the Egyptian monk, Antony. "All three of us were filled with wonder, we because the deeds we were now learning were so great, and he [the teller of the tale] because we had never heard them before."[19] Then came the revelation—dynamic in all languages and in all generations: *I saw, I heard, I beheld the glory of God!* It was the Holy Ghost at work among His people, drawing them to Him, through each other.

Now the final stage of the struggle begins. He suffered from "the pain of the new life coming to birth"[20] in him. The evidence is in: the historical verifications of the Biblical accounts, the witness of his friends, the testimony of the saints; and the hand of God upon him will not let him go. "Very well: now the truth is certain, yet you are still carrying the load. Here are men who have been given wings to free their shoulders from the load, though they did not wear themselves out in searching nor spend ten years or more thinking about it."[21] How this endears him to us, those of us who have likewise come to the vineyard in the eleventh hour!

His friend Alpius, also a skeptic, says to him: "What is wrong with us? . . . The unlearned arise and take heaven by force, and here we are with all our learning, stuck fast in flesh and blood!"[22] This is always the complaint of the intellectual when he begins to see what a cumbersome burden his mind has been to him. Why can't I be like others? Why do I have so much trouble coming to believe? Isn't this the way I feel?

Yet even when we clearly understand what we must do, we resist it; in the midst of our birth pangs we protest the departure of old Adam. How well I remember that last moment of Augustine's irresolution and torment in the garden just before his conversion, that last unavailing cry we all make, "Why this monstrousness? And what is the root of it? The mind gives the body an order, and is obeyed at once; the mind gives itself an order and is resisted. . . . "[23]

We simply cannot do what we have set ourselves to do, our will does not behave; we are beginning to discover that our will is far more apt in acquiring for ourselves what we want than what we don't want. At the moment of turning, the loss of what we want in ourselves is far more predominant than the prospect of what we are to gain.

How can we possibly know what our gain is to be, since we have not yet known God? We can think only of pleasures and delights we may have to renounce. It's all very well for those who have done it to liken our foolishness to the child who clutches his lollipops to his breast while he refuses to trade them for the pearl of great price, but it's not an easy thing to do. It is a moment fraught with real terror; we all come to sense in that moment that it is just the beginning of what shall be asked of us. God begins by asking for the lollipops. We do not yet know how He will help us, and so we are afraid of what more will be required of us.*

> . . . The nearer the point of time came in which I was to become different, the more it struck me with horror; but it did not force me utterly back nor turn me utterly away, but held me there between the two.[24]

We make our decision, the moment passes and, lo, everything is transformed. ". . . So that now it was a joy for me to renounce what I had been so afraid to lose."[25] And we weep

---

* Worse yet, we think we have to do this only once; fortunately we do not understand that we shall have to capitulate, renounce, surrender, and die to ourselves over and over again so long as we live. This is the condition of the new life and the means of its renewal. It is at once the deepest hardship and greatest happiness of the religious life.

with relief, as St. Augustine did under the tree, unabashedly, unashamedly. Now we can begin to learn about God through our own experience. With awe and reverence and love, we learn to fear Him; we learn to trust Him; we learn to worship Him. "I was in fear and horror, and again I was on fire with hope and exultation in Your mercy, O Father."[26] We learn to see God's purpose in our affairs. We also learn how certain we can be of Him—more sure even than of ourselves. "Yet I know something of You which I do not know of myself."[27]

But now a strange thing happens: all that was once, in that moment of truth, clear, unclouded, and transparent is now obscured. We don't notice it at first, we are hardly aware of it; we are content to drown in love. If anyone is so obtuse as to remind us of our duties, the problems we have left behind us, we are—in all sincerity—likely to ask, What problems? Or if we are prompted to concern ourselves with the affairs of the world, we are just as apt to exclaim, What world? It is a very lovely time, but fortunately it doesn't last forever.

Once he has found God, St. Augustine, too, becomes inarticulate. The fine, sharp edge of his mind is dulled, a fog descends, so that he now writes of nothing but his love for God. He moves in a stratum of delight, of rapture, of worship and praise—these, for the moment, are the only things worth mentioning. Later on his calm, his reason, and his understanding were restored to him; he could evaluate and judge; later he launched upon a dissertation of the Creation which is broad and incisive, but he never quite loses that stricken astonishment.

Perhaps the time will come when I, too, will see with clarity, and be able to come to conclusions about my own experience. Now I am still too near the time when I was mute with wonder, blinded by a light which—far from clarifying my own life—blurred even the nearest landmarks. I was like a weary traveler who wandered into a valley of overwhelming beauty. What would be my first act? To lament my disorientation and hurry on to more familiar ground, or to yield myself unwittingly to the splendor of my surroundings? One who finds himself in the habitation of the Most High is in no hurry to return to his own home! We are content not to know. "I continue not to know until my darkness shall be made as noonday in Your countenance."[28]

Thus God brings us out of our stupor and rapture; thus begins our long training in His service. St. Augustine's curiosity cannot long be silenced; like a giant, it must wake and stretch. Soon he is drawing upon all his senses, his reason, will, and "the huge court of my memory,"[29] eagerly to inquire into, to order, to subdue that which is, by its very nature, perfectly free. It is man's necessity to reckon with God on his own grounds regardless of how often he fails. St. Augustine does this without apology and with great vigor. That was the advantage of having been born in the fourth century A.D. We, in the twentieth, have been corrupted. We have become suspicious of our own efforts. In our sophistication we do not really believe that the power of God can become our own; we become hesitant and even cynical. Our faith is weakened.

Barely converted, and grieving over his mother's death, St. Augustine throws himself into a search in which he truly believes he can come fully to know himself and God. But we —we are they who "fall to what they can, and thus are content: because what they cannot do they do not want to do with sufficient intensity to make them able to do it."[30]

Apparently not even St. Augustine can continue indefinitely in his newly found assurance. He, too, becomes bewildered by his own questions, by his first efforts to please God. He has now to deal with the first fruits of scrupulosity.[31] He, too, feels the first chill when the joy to which he is accustomed disappears.[32] Ah, but it returns soon, so he is not yet in desolation; we who have come this way know what will be required of him, know what will be taken from him and given to him. It is like reading a story we have already read: we can anticipate each action before it occurs!

Unrelentingly he bares his faults, but pride seems not to be among them. It is both cheering and discouraging to the reader, both because we recognize ourselves in him and because we fail to do so. The sins of the saints can hardly be our own—no, I spoke too soon, he admits to pride. How curious that we can share every transgression with others: sloth, intemperance, morbidity, ingratitude, all the rest but pride. Somehow our pride always seems bigger and better than anyone else's!

Then St. Augustine, overwhelmed by the realization of his own unworthiness, feels separated from God. We all fall into the same pit. And he, too, seeks reconciliation as do we all, through the only Mediator—Christ.

Yet St. Augustine seems undaunted by his setbacks, and goes charging along like a rushing mountain stream, pure and graceful, determined by its very nature to reach the broad and all-encompassing sea. We see how his will pounds against the barricade, pulls away from all restraints imposed in his path by his flesh, overrides the dam that his reason erects, and, contrary to his very being, runs uphill when it must. I think, when the obstacles to faith are removed, we are all like that—tributaries, however small and sluggish, inexorably set upon reaching that deeper flood, that irresistible tide, that Spirit whose image we bear through the watermark of our baptism.

The search is a universal one, and common to all who have sought God. It is true of St. Augustine and of every Christian writer I have so far read—that is, when he writes of his own experience.

I think what pleases me most in St. Augustine is his modern, dynamic approach, which is more helpful to the skeptic than the more classical approach to God. St. Thomas Aquinas, for example, in representing the Churchman's point of view is static and loaded with hindsight. If you have been brought up in the Church, that which you so blithely assume *is* self-evident—but not so to the agnostic. Truth is not propositional —not when you are a pagan. When you start with nothing, you cannot with integrity assume anything. We who begin with doubt know from our own experience how little reason helps us at the start. As St. Augustine found, we must depend on the revelation of God: God revealing Himself through the Scriptures, through the arts, through His creation, through His children (first the chosen people of Israel, then the new remnant, the Christian family, the communion of saints) and, finally, through our own experience of Him.

This—a common Christian experience—is to me a far sounder argument for the existence of God, if that's what one requires, than all the so-called "proofs" based on reason. All they prove, as far as I can see, is that man can reason—which in itself reveals the hand of God more clearly than the process of man's reasoning, which often leads him astray. Seeing that men cannot agree among themselves about the reliability of simple sensory impressions, or the interpretation of empirical data, it is rather thrilling to see men, all starting from a different place and at a different time, arrive at the same point —not through reason, but through experience.

I never intended to get into such a book review, but I do

think that the *Confessions* ought to be on the best-seller list for converts! Before I close, I want to thank you for the little book of Psalms—I like the translation. How nice it must be to have a time set aside for worship, free of interruption! Surely even a layman can manage to outwit the demands and pressures about him and find moments here and there for prayer. I had to laugh at St. Teresa's comment about married people being too busy and involved to get beyond the first stage of prayer. Meditation over the dishes or a bathtub, which can serve as a *prie-dieu,* may not be ideal, but such meditation does serve.

Don't be alarmed, I shan't be sending you tomes like this very often. It was just that I found myself in a cul-de-sac; by writing it all down I was able to see where I was. Thanks for listening!

VII

Letter to Hugh

Reno, Nevada
November 22, 1957

Dear Hugh:

I have been promising to let you know how things stand with me in my growth as a Christian. So much has happened that it does not seem possible that I was confirmed only a year and a half ago! In some ways I seem to have made great strides, in others to have stood still—or rather, to have gone in a circle and come back to where I once stood. I suspect a circular type of growth is not uncommon, rather like a tree that adds a ring.

I tried to deal with the "first things" of Christian morality, but gave it up, and went on to other things; now I am back where I was before. For a long while I was busy acquiring belief—a working faith, and becoming acquainted with the Church. That led me to a real experience with God; as the Scriptures could have taught me: "If thou wouldest believe, thou shouldest see the glory of God."[1]

Now I am undertaking to mix a little Martha in with my Mary, to turn a cutting edge into a little grain; but coming by any harvest is discouraging, and I am grateful for a sense of humor that permits me to laugh at my own audacity.

I caught myself saying the other day, "Oh, my Father, forgive me for counting my virtues, but they're the first ones

I've ever had!" And they are. Although I had parentally and socially conditioned good behavior, when I entered the Church I had no virtue, and at first I thought to acquire some—not so much out of shame of self or love of God, but more out of expediency. When we move into a splendid new home and bring with us our old belongings, we are not unaware of the contrast, and there is a certain amount of what-will-the-neighbors-think mixed in; but beyond all that was a conviction that having embraced the faith it behooved me to acquire the fruit. Not only should I think and feel and believe as a Christian, but I should also behave like one. I erred in assuming the latter to be a natural outcome of the former. Well, perhaps it is, but it does not follow as the day the night. Virtue is God-begotten, grace-given, and hard-won.

I thought I was going to be able to devote this letter to an intelligent discussion of such Christian values, since that is your chief interest, but I see that I am not. I cannot yet draw any conclusions in the moral field; instead I will have to be content with description. Anything more will have to wait until I achieve a vantage point or perhaps make another full circle of growth. But you, having come this way yourself, will be able to see where I stand.

The best I can say is that I have at long last made some visible progress in understanding the relation of God and man; even though it is a small crop of turnips (a most unseemly vegetable!) I'm pleased with it. I think we have a right to be glad and grateful for any progress we make in this direction. If we can honestly discern a moral gain, it is a cause for thanksgiving. I am not proud of the delays, the rationalizations, the bumblings and the fumblings, but I am proud of what God hath wrought in the unlikely climate of my heart. After I have a more abundant crop, I may cease to be amazed; I may even learn how to take it all for granted.

I remember the book you gave me on Christian morality referred specifically to the cardinal virtues. I read only two chapters in it and then I lost it; since I was loath to admit of so strict a discipline, it was an excellent means of avoiding the obligation of reading it. Later, nearly a year after we moved here, I searched for it. Now I am writing to ask you for the title and author so I can get another copy. I am curious to see what it was all about.

I think I already know. The very idea of undertaking to alter my life in any way, to change my opinions, values, and behavior, was an unnerving one and it remained so until recently. At first I didn't think it would be necessary. Even philosophical discussions of ethics bored me, but when it came to a practical consideration of morality it would all start to sound Bunyanesque and I was able to smile tolerantly. I had a fairly active conscience, but I've discovered that the old saying that it is the Voice of Authority is not necessarily true. A conscience can be conditioned by something other than God. It can be shaped by puritanical parents, by frustrated teachers, by the mores of culture or people—none of which is necessarily Christian. And, too, conscience can easily be the means by which we rationalize our desires.

To leave for a moment the matter of acquiring virtue and consider the matter of serving God—how can it be best accomplished? What are the techniques of living a Christian life? Obviously there are some things I'm never going to be capable of and others that I shall have to learn to acquire. But there is my particular *attrait*, what I can best do, shaped by my personality and background, limited by my capacities. It seems to me that it is not sensible to abandon this for other talents, even if I could master what is foreign to my nature. I no longer bemoan my lack of simplicity. My response to God is mixed and complex: at times mystical, at times practical, and at times intellectual.

Let's look at those three approaches in four outstanding servants of God. In St. Teresa the mystical is predominant; her love of God and desire for spiritual union with Him overcame all other approaches. It intensifies, as well as limits, her capacities. In her single-hearted, single-minded, headlong search for God we find a force that is absent in people burdened with more human and practical restraints. She repeatedly states that, given her own natural inclination, she would have no contact with people at all save those who were necessary to the advancement of her soul—namely, her priest and confessor. She shrinks from people who are "wretched," she finds her kinsmen "wearisome," eating and drinking are regrettable necessities, she desires only to die that she might be with God fully. Yet in spite of her personal limitations she makes some remarkably practical achievements by founding new Orders and reforming older ones.

Quite a contrast to St. Francis who finds his love and service of God in pestholes and among the poor and leprous, and whose compassion for the natural order, men and animals, leaves us with hymns of praise and canticles of rejoicing. Yet the very time spent in those pursuits, however holy, limited him. That he was, for the most part, in the world, and that St. Teresa was cloistered, are facts which color their responses.

Then let us consider another practical approach: that of Evelyn Underhill, whose *Fruits of the Spirit, The Light of Christ,* and *Abba* I have read recently. What a different working edge she turns to God! Faithful, humble service in daily affairs, the tedious and lowly acceptance of God's will, the discharge of duties, the offering up of self out of the midst of a busy life. Yet she is limited because she can only contemplate the mysteries of God; she cannot enter into them fully.

Or take the more intellectualized approach of St. Augustine. We miss at times some of the vivid warmth and passionate outpouring of self, yet we find an insight that is clear and bright and revealing, the insight of a brilliant scholar whose careful and inspired efforts bring us to the very threshold of Truth.

As we cannot be all things to all men, so we cannot, even at our best, in the most notable opportunities for human service, give more than a small part of ourselves to God. By definition and by experience, we find that to develop and perfect one aspect of our service is to neglect another. When we see that even the saints have feet of clay we must remember that only the Son of God has been able to utilize all aspects of His humanity in the service of the Father, and that His saints —those known and unknown—have in this world courageously undertaken to follow His example.

So it was on All Saints' Day that I loosed my anxious hold on what I had reserved for myself and withheld from others, and gave myself into His hands. Nearly a month has passed since my act of dedication and, if nothing else, I am closer to an understanding of our Lord's words which have always baffled me: "My yoke is easy, and my burden is light."[2] The moment of surrender is crowned with a serenity and poise I did not think possible—for myself. But it is not so astonishing when you consider the amount of friction and division that is thereby avoided. The efforts to serve both God and man can create serious dichotomies. How much energy is now available that was formerly expended in such struggles! How much more time I have, now that it is no longer neces-

sary to spend it wholesale in protecting my pride, rationalizing my inadequacies, finding supports for my weaknesses and
outlets for my needs. (Those who have never done this on a
full-scale basis have no idea how time-consuming it can be!)
How free I am from hurt and disappointment now that I need
less and less of what I once thought so necessary to my comfort and happiness. A complex desire system can be extremely
frustrating, and any attempt to integrate many-sided demands
results inevitably in serious disharmony.

Even more to the point, how many times will I have to
learn this? And why won't what I learn stay learned? Does it
for you? It takes so long for an insight to become a hindsight.
First I must appraise, then accept, and finally act; then I must
start all over again and appraise, accept, and act upon the act.

Perhaps I do lament my lack of simplicity, after all!

Ash Wednesday, 1958

This letter has been long a-borning. So much has been
done and undone, then redone again; learned, unlearned, and
relearned. But my growing edge creeps forward. This is the
wonder of growing in God, unilateral though it seems at
times. Any other relationship would have long since died out;
but God knows how much pressure we can bear, and He
promises us not only that we shall not be tempted beyond
ourselves, but also that His grace will be sufficient.

Recently I became separated from God again. As before,
the estrangement grew out of trivial things, once more barrenness and isolation drove me to acts of despair, once again
the channel of prayer seemed closed to me and, like King
Claudius in *Hamlet,* I felt that "My words fly up, my thoughts
remain below." I was once more earth-bound and world-ori-

ented. I bitterly resented being crept up on, so to speak. I asked why we are not permitted to know in advance, before separation takes place, that it is imminent. At least we would have a chance to put up a decent fight! But, then, we'd all be heroes and Christianity would be something we'd attain without loving Christ.

Once I saw this for what it was, I desperately reminded myself that I must above all remember what I had learned from my first experience: to continue in my habitual contacts with God, with or without emotional reward, for as long as necessary. I did this doggedly for a while, but it was plain that it was something I had learned by rote and that I had not yet developed an unquestioned and automatic response. Perhaps only the saints are capable of immediate obedience, but because I still expected too much of myself I was impatient and disgusted with my behavior. And there went my small crop of turnips—hardly above ground and already blighted! I complained that it simply wasn't fair, scarcely to get under way only to be cut down. How I had longed for some visible evidence of inward grace! It's all very well to tell yourself that pride goeth before a fall, that I was trying too hard, that I should "let go and let God" and all that, but it simply doesn't work. One might as well save his breath. (I heard a dandy definition of a platitude the other day: it is something that one has heard but not experienced.)

I did discover one thing: my earlier loss of contact with God did not go for nothing. Having once experienced the loss I was able to recognize the symptoms quite promptly and so the whole period of crisis was lessened. The impact was softened by experience and I did not panic, nor did I tumble back into skepticism and disbelief. My faith held on, and I did not stumble.

The last time I brought my separation to an end by confession. (By the way, it was the first time I had ever made a formal confession.) Again it has proved to be the means of restoration. This, followed by Holy Communion, set me right. There has been no emotional release, the channel of prayer is not fully opened to me, and there is not the slightest evidence that I have been forgiven, that I am no longer separated from God. How do I know the restoration is true? Because, having done everything I could, I know that I must take God at His word. If I have learned anything, I have learned that His word is always, unfailingly, reliable. I must drink of Him even when He does not quench my thirst.

Sooner or later my will must give way to His. And even when there is no comfort in that, I can still rejoice in it because, and only because, it is His will.

I know now what my next step must be: I must learn how to be able to lose contact with God without becoming separated from Him. Let me explain. Last summer I was convinced that we ourselves, with the co-operation of evil—the Devil, if you will—brought about the separation from God. I am still convinced of it. God Himself does not discipline us that way. Separation is not sin, and our Lord never wills us to be cut off from Him. But what *causes* separation is something quite different: the loss of contact with God, the loss of the sustaining joy that makes all our obligations to Him their own reward. When we lose this, people like myself feel that our Father has forsaken us, and we leave God like spoiled children in a temper tantrum.

God does seem to withhold the fullness of His love from time to time, but we grow as a result of it. It deepens our love for Him, increases our capacities in His service, humbles us, hones us, perfects us. At a time when we are likely to forget it, He reminds us that it is His will that we must further. When we need it, He lets us know that He is the only "All" we have to have. The actual separation is left up to us.

February 20, 1958

Now it is time again to ask myself the familiar question: how does one ever manage to live a Christian life? I simply do not know. Virtue does not come naturally to me. But, you protest, it doesn't with anyone. Yes, I realize that because of original sin one is not born virtuous. But with many Christians virtue reaches a level where it operates almost automatically and effortlessly, and sometimes habitually. I cannot even sin with any degree of spontaneity! Now I have to make cross references, check and double check; I feel as if I were learning a kind of Dewey Decimal System. If only virtue could be a matter of black/white, either/or, then my choices would be immensely simplified. But now I find I must make new kinds of distinctions in my value judgments. All this used to be very stimulating on a theoretical level, but on a practical basis it's a laborious affair. It can no longer be, for me, a merely logical exercise; now it involves a new way of life which would satisfy a charity I do not yet possess and a discipline of which I am not yet capable.

Perhaps the book you gave me, which I cannot find, would tell me. I doubt it, however. Although I can't seem to make the Christian way mine, I doubt if reading anything on the level of principle would help. If there were anything written out of human experience which tells act by act how it is accomplished, I might know. But my reading shows that what is offered is so full-blown it is nearly useless to me. That is why the experience I had at Camp Galilee last summer was so valuable to me; over a dozen of us formed a "workshop" and discussed in daily sessions a point-by-point consideration of Christian morality. Perhaps I ought to try to get a discussion group going in our parish. I am sure there must be others who need to share actual experiences and receive practical instruction.

I am learning that in the moral field of religion I have to feel my way. First of all, there is more to religion than morality, although some people talk as if the latter were the sum and substance. When St. Thomas Aquinas says: "In this then consists our blessedness, that we be obedient to God," I cannot entirely agree with him. Certainly we must be obedient to God; but if our blessedness depends only upon our obedience, we are in a pretty bad fix. The Gospel proclaims that it is not man but God who redeems and blesses us—not because we are good, but because God loves us. Our blessedness consists in this: that God loves us. How else can we explain the fact that in the midst of doubt, rebellion, and sin He showers upon us His gifts of grace?

This we have to discover for ourselves. Our obedience, no less than anything else, depends largely upon a living life of prayer. Prayer is our chief contact with God, and I am discovering that when prayer is neglected all the avenues of grace become jammed. Each must learn for himself through experience how much prayer he requires in order to sustain his life in God. I think it varies a great deal from individual to individual. The saints, those athletes who are most rigorously trained in the service of God, require the most. It is like eating food: each person needs a different amount. A laborer doing heavy work needs far more calories than a scholar whose physical activities are rather limited. A child needs more protein; an adolescent has needs totally different from those of an older person. So it is with prayer: not only do our needs vary but our needs vary from stage to stage, from time to time.

In our beginnings, once we discover the joy and the strength that can be found in prayer, we pray frequently and nothing seems able to restrain us. After we reach that stage, prayer grows difficult, and we find that there are times when we have to exercise the will—to force ourselves to pray, to keep from becoming spiritually weakened. Later, we learn that during a crisis constant prayer is necessary.

Some days our souls are nourished by frequent, spontaneous outpourings, an almost involuntary cry that fulfills a mysterious yearning within us. Other days we express ourselves in more formal or patterned prayers. Sometimes it subdues our anger, our querulousness, our childish pique, our hatred and despair. Sometimes prayer is liturgical, as in a Church service, and can be quite satisfying. At other times we stammer out our needs, sometimes selfishly, sometimes in behalf of others. Sometimes a mechanical recitation is all that we can muster. At other times the gladness of our hearts wells up into the glorious language of thanksgiving.

Prayer is painful, it is rewarding, it is an empty abstraction, it is serene and contemplative, it is abortive and hasty, it is a communion of fellowship, it is self-consciously devout, it is animate with energy, power, vitality, it leaps beyond the self and penetrates the outer rim of heaven, it is communion with God.

Prayer is many-sided, as are all communications with others, but it is far more varied than any conversation because it involves not only our own human traits but the divine attributes of an infinite Personality. It is unbelievable, long after it becomes evident; but, to a religious person, it is, in some form or another, absolutely necessary. We know how people who are removed from their fellow men live in a dark and dismal world. How much more empty are the lives of those who would depend upon God, but who are yet without prayer! When we cease to pray, we cease to live. I know now that prayer is far more necessary, vital, and urgent than good works, virtue, or obedience to God. All those things depend on prayer; indeed, our whole relationship to God is sustained chiefly by this form of communication, be it devotion and adoration, petition and thanksgiving, intercession, or confession.

Yet in prayer, as in all our contacts with God, most of our suppositions seem to be based upon a ready assumption of joy. If we can pray for our own reasons and give God the credit for it, we rest assured. But sometimes some of us stop to ask an embarrassing question: is it really done to the glory of God, or to our own ends? In a terrible moment, we see that our own will is not always consonant with the will of God. My statement of that discovery seems to be commonplace enough. It is the kind of thinking that is often found in books on religious morality; yet when we really encounter the principle of God-versus-us in our life, it begins to have an impact that cannot be duplicated by our reading or our second-hand experiences.

There is so little in us that is like God. When we find His Image in us—and it *is* there—we hold it to the light, marveling. But as a rule we find it a flashing, ephemeral thing, here and gone, taken and assumed and quickly lost. When we do not have it we forget that we ever had it. When we have it momentarily we nearly always assume that it comes from us and is of our own making.

Above all, we take it for granted; if we think about it at

all we presume that God wills us to serve Him only with joy. Only later do we discover that our first assumption is not always true—and then we abandon God. I say this forcefully because I did. Almost all of us do if we go even a little way toward knowing Him. Abandoning Him seems to be part of learning to know Him, but it is a time of fierce and gnawing remorse; a time when we think we may have made a mistake; a time when we are ready to die for almost any cause except the slow, sure demand that is placed upon us by Him who said that we would have to go this way. We always want it otherwise—our way—and the further we go the more we learn that it cannot be in any way that is satisfactory, flattering, or a cause of facile rejoicing to us.

As we pray, we find that at first almost everything we ask for comes to us: it is a kind of "beginner's luck" that God permits us until He winds us in His labyrinthine ways. I, for one, am never certain. I, for one, reject His ways and look sometimes for a new Messiah, a less difficult way. But I, for one, have learned that this sweet mercy is bought at a cost and that if we have once become involved in His design we never afterwards really have a choice.

For those of us who want our own will or our own way, Christianity is a disastrous path: it will bring us more suffering than we ever thought possible. But, with patience, it will bring us a love-bearing, thirst-quenching joy that transforms life. It is an enigma, not to be sought after for those who love rational certainty; even for those who crave experience it is a questionable and perilous route. It is God: the ultimate Mystery.

I have lately been thinking more about the Sacraments and feel that in many Episcopal parishes the Sacrament of Penance has been disregarded. I agree that sacramental confession is not obligatory, but I do feel that it should be explained and made available to every member of the Church. Parish priests (and bishops) simply do not know how ignorant their people are!

Like you, I was confirmed in the South. Although some mention was made of sacramental confession during my confirmation instructions, as a matter of practice it never amounted to anything more than a chat with the priest. That, however, was due as much to my hesitation as to my ignorance; had I specifically asked to make my confession, I'm sure I would have been accommodated. But many people, especially those who come into the Church from Protestant bodies, find the thought of confessing their sins to a priest embarrassing; others, not aware of the Catholic tradition of the Church, consider it a rather Romish custom.

There is an inconceivable difference, however, between having a talk with a clergyman and making one's confession to a priest. In the first place, the clergyman is at best a friend and any advice that he offers, however excellent, cannot answer one's deepest needs. Since it is a personal relationship, there is a tendency to observe amenities, to minimize, to couch one's words in casual phrases, to make one's self "look good." But the relationship of priest to penitent in the confessional is utterly impersonal. It is not only that the confessional seal assures secrecy, but also, with its sacramental character, the relationship is not a person-to-person association and the priest is not a mere man acting on his own, but—and this is important—he stands in the stead of Christ.

Whatever one's personal attitude may be, the fact remains that confession is one of the seven Sacraments of the Church, and I feel that if each person who presents himself for membership were only told not only *of* it but also *about* it, sacramental confession would become a natural part of a congregation's very life, and those of us who now hesitate would not be timid in availing ourselves of its incomparable spiritual and therapeutic values. I have found many members of our Church who do not even know that the Sacrament exists.

When I came here, I knew of its existence, that there was such a Sacrament, but I did not know how one went about using it, in what it consisted, or how it was dispensed. I had been a member of the Church for over a year before my own inner need drove me to make inquiries. Still rather vague about some aspects of Church history, I began to wonder if the Sacrament of Penance belonged, perhaps, to the Church of England and other Anglican Churches but, for some reason, not to the Episcopal Church, for after all, I had never known anyone in our Church to make a formal confession. Early last summer, when I first experienced separation from God, I decided to find out for once and for all whether or not it was available to me, not only theoretically but actually. I asked our Bishop and was happily relieved to find that it was, and so I was promptly instructed in its meaning and use.

During the last seven months I have availed myself of the Sacrament of Confession several times. Occasionally, as the first time, I was so overwhelmed by my own sense of guilt that the General Confession in the public services of the Church failed to bring about any feeling of restoration. Sometimes I wanted to start all over, and voicing my resolutions and seeing my failures gave me all the impetus I needed. Sometimes my need moved outside myself and I not only felt a desire to be reconciled with God Himself but, since I had in a particular way offended against my fellow men, I needed to be reconciled to them also. Sometimes self-examination became uncertain, my conscience dulled, contrition crippled. Sometimes I wanted to know in a definite and realistic way that I had been absolved—actually forgiven. It is only through the Sacrament of Penance that I found what I wanted, and what I needed—the removal of all that separated me from God.

My mind keeps coming back to certain theological problems which I'd like to clarify for myself. One of them is the recurring problem of evil, and I'd like to consider it in the framework of the Garden of Eden.

I don't believe the Fall, original sin, or whatever you want to call it, lay so much in the things we like to think it did. I don't believe it was so much that man was tempted, that it was human nature to want forbidden fruit, that he was tempted by the fruit itself because it was ripe, glossy, and fragrant; or even that he was doomed to disobedience; or that he wanted to gain experience. All this may be true, of course, for we are a curious people. It's true that sin is often attractively packaged. Also man is, I'll grant you, lured into the penumbra of experience: that's how he rationalizes his vices, that he will "learn something." I think God chose the Jews as a race to which He could reveal Himself because they were especially curious about the unknown, because they were a "peculiar people."

But I don't believe evil arose so much out of the things I have just mentioned as out of man's desire to "be like God, knowing good and evil.'"[3] It is such a subtle sin that it almost always escapes detection. It is grounds for sin because it can be both good and evil, for it enables man to have a clearer conception of good, as well as a more intimate knowledge of evil. Can you imagine the vacuity of man's experience in the Garden of Eden? Knowing nothing of what he lacked (I'm rather doubtful of the argument that he lacked nothing), we can only presume that man was as happy as his innocence permitted him to be. We tend to romanticize man's earliest existence, to forget that, although he was without knowledge of evil, he was also without full knowledge of good and thus was deprived of any possibility of *understanding* God. The cheering, and at the same time chilling, thought is that man can make the same choice all over again, any day of the week. I can. The ability or endowment to choose is, and always has been, man's distinguishing characteristic; it is what separates him from all other creatures.

It's a frightening thing to realize that we are able to murder our husbands, spoil our children, defame our neigh bors, blaspheme God, and destroy ourselves, and that we are restrained only by the slimmest tether to our nature—our being good as well as evil. The full recognition of all the implications of free will is so unnerving that we lose our stability; we panic, we shake our fist at God for having so limited us, and we end up by blaming Him for evil. We behave like children who, having deserted the security of their parents and run headlong into disaster, would have their parents be responsible for all the consequences. We think it loving and kind for a parent to assume the blame. But God does not allow this, because the very growth stimulated by independent action is thwarted unless we can deal also with the results of that action. Pure and simple dependence on God ended when we made our ancient choice. Now we are faced with the problem of good and evil. When God seemed to exist apart from His creatures there was no problem at all; the problem arose only when man moved into an entirely new relationship with his Creator, a relationship that allowed him not only to find and know God, but to lose and deny Him.

In Dorothy Sayers' magnificent portrayal of the life of Christ, *The Man Born to Be King*,[4] she gives us a portrait of Judas that I find fascinating. It is also disturbing, because it shows us a picture of ourselves—man in whom good-become-evil turns upon itself. Here is a man, she tells us, who was talented and intelligent; he understood Jesus better than the other Disciples, and he made good use of his talents for his Master. But, being capable of so much goodness, he was equally (perhaps more?) capable of so much evil; for there was another side of the coin—pride, malice, greed, and above all, his desire to mastermind the whole project. He wanted, in other words, "to be like God."[5] He became convinced that Jesus didn't know what He was up to; he grew disillusioned when he saw that the promised Kingdom was not being brought about so soon and so forcefully as he had hoped; he felt that he, Judas, could do a much better job of it if he were given half a chance! When he began to doubt the validity of the Messianic claims, his disintegration commenced.

Here, I think, lies the meaning of the "unforgivable sin": here is the old contest between the two irreconcilable parts of nature, the point at which man, having found and known God, denies and loses Him. Of course, the question then arises: how does St. Peter differ from Judas, since he, too, denied our Lord? St. Peter's act was transient, Judas' irrevocable. St. Peter denied, yes, but he still believed that Jesus had the power to forgive him. Judas, because he saw himself as God, could not, despite his remorse, be restored, because he no longer believed that Jesus had the power of absolution—a power, as our Lord points out, greater than that of healing or raising from the dead. Forgiveness is the greater miracle.

February 22, 1958

Today Father Bart was ordained a priest. It was the first ordination I had ever witnessed. I was not prepared to be overwhelmed by so much beauty, dignity, and holiness. It reminded me of the consecration of our camp chapel, St. John's-in-the-Wilderness, last summer, except that that service pertained only to a house of God, and today's to the setting apart of a human representative of Christ on earth as pastor, prophet, and priest. It made me proud to be a member of the Episcopal Church. On such occasions we comprehend most fully what it means to be a member of the Holy Catholic Church, a cell in the Mystical Body of Christ. At such a time we come nearest to understanding the words of the *Sanctus:* the Lord God of hosts, whom, with Angels and Archangels, with all the company of heaven, we laud and magnify. It is truly "meet and right" so to do.

What variety our Church houses! It has all the elements of our "bounden duty" and answers our deepest needs. This week is a good example: beginning with Morning Prayer, the recitation of psalms, canticles, petitions, and thanksgivings; moving on to Ash Wednesday and the beginning of the great penitential season of Lent, inviting both the willing and the unwilling to cry aloud for God's mercy; then on to the evening Litany in which a worshipping and supplicating congregation move from the desire for contrition to the act of penitence; developing on Friday morning where only three of us gathered together under a rain-rattled roof and humbly participated in a simple celebration of Holy Communion; culminating in today's, Saturday's, ordination. These were only five services and it was only one week out of the Church Year, but each one expressed man's many-sided need of God: his yearning for repentance, confession, forgiveness, and restoration; his need for petition, intercession, thanksgiving, worship, and adoration.

Occasionally we grow restive and bored; we criticize the Church (thank God we have the right to!), and some of us have the gumption to suggest constructive changes. In thinking back over my limited experience in the Anglican Communion I am impressed with her diversity and flexibility, her extensive ministry. To be a rock that will not move, and at the same time a growing thing that must move, is quite something.

The Church is human only so far as her members are human: she is in reality a Divine Organism, unlimited by time and space; although a part of that Divine Organism, we human beings err, and by our nature are limited; but the Church by her nature can restore us to the Mystical Body of Christ, just as she grafted us into that Body in the first place by our baptism; and by that grafting, that restoration, we too, by the grace of God, can grow out of the limits of our humanity and into the larger life of the Church Expectant and the glory of the Church Triumphant.

And so, quite unexpectedly, I was again caught up into that exultation that can never be earned, sought after, or even prayed for, but like our redemption is a gift freely given to them that love God. It is to be lifted out of ourselves into an area where we are one with all humankind, a brotherhood of joy. This is indeed a brotherhood of joy, a mighty wind that cannot be resisted, an abundance that cannot be contained but must spill over into the lives of all who touch us. It is a lesson we must learn to translate into acts of love. It is a bottomless stream from which we drink and are refreshed in the midst of the dull and commonplace. It is provision and pasture, the grapes of glory clustering on the vine. It is a mystery in which we, all unwittingly, pivot upon ourselves and turn our face to God.

But what does all this have to do with our daily living? Translated into terms of attitudes and activities, this is how we behave when we are filled with that loving responsiveness to God: our awareness of beauty is heightened; all of nature is sharpened in texture and tone; colors are brightened; nuances which before escaped us appear before our eager eyes. We see things as an artist, as Croce might have—content not to capture it on canvas or in clay, but to receive it into ourselves with quiet gratitude.

Before, we might have been shy or awkward with people, but now we are capable of graceful response. Unthinkingly we reach out to people and draw them to us. In small encounters we realize we are no longer acting within the confines of our habitual self-interest, but are driven outward to others—not merely in respectable, but in inspired, acts of charity and concern. The neighbor whom we could not tolerate we greet affectionately; a relationship which was taken for granted becomes precious.

Released from inhibitions and fatigue, we can now accomplish our work with ease and efficiency. Disagreeable and onerous tasks are approached as opportunities to express our gratitude. We lovingly dedicate ourselves with broom and mop, pen and ink, and all the tools of our trade.

There is fresh insight into everything. We understand things which were before obscure, whether in Scripture or in the daily newspaper. We exclaim, with delight or with distress, "So this is how things stand!" Where we once had only glimpses into reality, we now enjoy a continuous comprehension.

And there is laughter and gaiety of spirit. Whether in the subtle humor of a bon mot or in clowning with the children, we enjoy the Psalmist's "merriment of God."

We are fortified with courage. We wonder again if somewhere there isn't a mountain we can move. We have a touch of the martyr's strength. A capacity for suffering beyond our imagination is now conceivable through this blessing.

Before, our worship and praise were often languid, distracted, or self-conscious, but now with the "whole man" we can unashamedly give full voice to our adoration and thanksgiving.

All this (and many other types of response, depending upon the person) is what a Christian sooner or later becomes familiar with. Now I can see the answer to my earlier problem, when I protested that virtue did not come naturally to me, and that I had to work at it. I had asked myself how any of this could become habitual in one to whom it was so foreign. How is commandment translated into responsive action?

Perhaps this problem isn't a universal one; perhaps people don't, by and large, find the difficulty I do in thinking, in feeling, and in behaving as our Lord said we must. I suppose if you learn how to walk only after you are full grown you have to deal with a set of circumstances entirely different from that of the infant candidate. People speak, it seems to me rather glibly, of imitating Christ. I have often wondered how we can know if we are doing that. It is not simply a matter of expanding the best that is within us; new values must be added, new dimensions perceived. Yet even when that is accomplished the Son of Man outdoes us, not just in quantity, but in a quality of response that is not found in the human race.

I now realize that we are not left to work this out "by the book"—as a lesson to be learned, for to those who ask for the gift of the Holy Spirit this new dimension is given. Through us it is demonstrated; we ourselves experience it. We can, thus blessed, know what it is to be released from our limitations so that we may know and remember what love and courage are like, and in a time of barrenness be assured of the abundance which surrounds us on all sides. We cannot live perpetually in that boundless way, but looking through the eyes of Christ we can learn more in a single moment than in many months of selfish struggling. When we try to do it ourselves we masquerade, but when God is with us we come "not as a stranger."

That this rhythm of experience applies to our intellectual inquiries as well as to our strivings to live the Christian life is one more proof that God's truth is active and dynamic—a personal, living thing, and not a set of static, impersonal propositions. It lends to all our intellectual researches in the theological field a faint air—not perhaps of triviality—but of failing to get to grips. It pushes us back from study to prayer, from our chair at the desk onto our knees before the altar. Above all, I think, it adds to the deep gravity of our theological argument, to our vehement denunciations of heresy and error, a faint echo of divine laughter—laughter neither derisive nor ironic, but tranquil, rich, well-pleased. That we should have followed such a long, such an arduous course, in order to arrive at this simple living contact with him who gives himself to the wise and simple, the learned and the unlettered, in like fullness and abundance![6]

It may be my earlier script-writing training that makes this letter sound so much like the perils of Pauline—another cliff-hanging episode in which we are invited to return next week to see whether Donet makes the grade! The fact is that it's no longer a precarious experience, grounded in myself, and nourished by my own hope. Whatever I do, or fail to do, my life can never again be the same. My behavior may not be constant, but I know that I have reached the point where I can never again act without reckoning with that act. When we have found God, we have no other choice. When Jesus asked His Disciples if they would also leave Him, St. Peter responded, as we all must, "Lord, to whom shall we go? thou hast the words of eternal life."[7]

By the way, I found the book you gave me: it is *Fortitude and Temperance*, by Josef Pieper.[8] I found it in the bookcase in the study. Putting a book there is the surest way I know to lose it! I'll send you my reaction to it when I'm farther into it, but let me say this now: I have a growing suspicion of any approach that attempts to codify morality. When we confine virtue, or the lack of it, to any given framework, we may be tempted to leave it there, and this, as J. B. Phillips points out, makes of Christianity a performance rather than an experience.

Your godchildren send you their love. Some random comments—from Mark: "My skin feels so nice and comfortable!" —from Meredith: "Mommy, this is a do-it-yourself egg!" (An egg in the shell.) I continually learn from them. One evening during Meredith's prayers (after I had been struggling all day with the whole matter of the will of God) she gave me one in her words: " . . . And let us be happy as long as we can, and when we can't, let us not be too angry."

Thank you for waiting so patiently for this grew-like-Topsy letter.

VIII

Letter to My Relatives

Christmas Day, 1958

Dear Lois, Charmian, and Lynn:*

It was Saturday evening, December 20. Dad was visiting us for Christmas. I had been awakened the night before with violent cramps; the doctor had come and gone with threats of hospitalization for observation of an irritable appendix. In view of the Christmas season I prevailed upon him to let me be observed at home. I decided I *must* be well by the following Tuesday when we were planning a large Christmas open house, with a guest list of over thirty people.

This was how things stood when a call came that was to change all of our lives and suck us into a horror that is almost unbelievable. The call was from a neighbor in Alhambra who told us that Mother had been shot and killed. We had only recently learned from Dad that Candace's former boy friend (whom I will here call "Stan") had refused to take "no" for an answer when she broke off with him a couple of months ago, and had been writing her threatening letters and making ominous phone calls. Thoroughly alarmed, Dad had put the matter in the hands of the police and a restraining order was issued. There was some police surveillance, but really very

---

* This letter was taken from a larger letter written to my mother's nearest relatives who asked to be informed of the frightful events surrounding her death.

little could be done until something had been done, so to speak.

It seems that Stan had come to the house that evening with the express purpose of killing my sister (an intention he had been overheard to express in a bar a few evenings before). When she answered the door, he leaped at her; she screamed and Mother came running in. Mother was apparently shot when she tried to intervene to protect Candace. Then followed a harrowing fifteen minutes or so in which Candace dashed about the house trying to escape him. Another man, Harry, her date for the evening, arrived on the scene, grappled with Stan, and, trying to disarm him, was shot twice in the head. (The wounds proved to be superficial and he was later released from the hospital.) Harry managed to get next door and phoned the police. (We certainly owe a debt of gratitude to Harry. Can you imagine what courage it must have taken— after hearing the volley of shots and knowing what the situation was—deliberately to rush into it?)

Harry got Stan out of the house, but he managed to get back in by smashing in the windows. When his further attempts to kill Candace were unsuccessful, he tried to shoot himself; when that failed (he had run out of bullets) he slashed his wrists. It was then that the police arrived and attempted to get him out of the house (Candace had by then managed to run next door with Harry), but he plunged a kitchen knife into his abdomen. Incredible as it sounds, he lived—and is recovering.

Mother was shot in the heart and in the arm. She had time to say, "He shot me" before she fell to the floor in the hallway. Then a few moments later she cried out, "I am dying! Run, Candace, run!" Candace cannot be sure just when Mother died, but it couldn't have been more than a short while afterwards; she was pronounced dead when the ambulance arrived along with the police minutes later. (I think we were all forced to consider how she would have hated to linger through a long terminal illness, which was certainly possible, considering her age and how terribly hard she'd been working.) Candace miraculously escaped with a head laceration and glass cuts on her arms. For a while we thought she had been killed too. It seemed like a macabre nightmare, and none of us could quite manage to grasp it. Until it was time for Dad to be taken to the airport to catch the next plane back, we sat around in stunned silence.

The familiar feeling of shock descended; the last time I had experienced it (apart from our dog Fricka's violent death) was when Meredith, at two years, had fallen on her head from a second-story porch to the concrete below. While waiting for the X-rays at the hospital I had the same awkward sense of numbed detachment, seeing everything painfully clearly but feeling as though it had nothing to do with me.

I wept nearly all of Sunday. By then, after phone calls making plans for Mother's funeral, I "woke up." I am ashamed to say that my first reaction was one of panic. It was the old childish pattern of escape—avoid pain at any cost. It was the same old flight I had taken so many times before. It was what had kept me from becoming deeply involved with other people —the fear of being hurt. I did not want to go to California, to the grim things that awaited me there. I almost prayed for my appendix to burst. Oh, to be so restrained by circumstances that my cowardice might not be known! The life of a craven is not an easy one. When you, Charmian, said on the phone that night that you thought I was being brave, I really cringed. If you had only known!

It was all mixed in with other terrors with which I had

not fully come to grips: the nameless dread that has its origin in childhood, "the dark at the top of the stairs," the fear of being totally liable, utterly vulnerable to whatever comes, the mouse in the jaws of the cat. It is compounded of shrinking from the unknown, of death—your own, but more especially that of others—of pain that cannot be borne, of pressure that cannot be resisted. It is what we never discuss, even with our closest friends. It is the badge of the coward; the mark of him who, no matter how many strides may have been made, is still not mature.

Without my faith I could never have undertaken to go. Without my belief that God would somehow sustain me, I would have run fast and far in the other direction. Heaven only knows where I would have hidden—I have so few hiding places left—or to what extent I could have rationalized everything. But those are all academic matters. The following day Bob and I flew high over the Sierras bound for my family home.

Dad had a shock going home that early morning, almost as great as the one my sister had suffered. Since it wasn't certain just when he would arrive, it had been agreed that he would phone Candace from the airport and she would have someone meet him. She had gone over to a friend's house and had requested his telephone answering service to call her there—the idea being to prevent his going home to that gruesome scene. But the answering service failed to relay the message and he did just that. Somehow his opening his door on all of that shakes me more than anything that went before.

First Candace and then Dad bore the brunt of what had happened. When we got there the bloodstains from Stan's attempted suicide had been largely scrubbed away, and the broken glass was for the most part carted off. We were all left with the less grisly but more heartbreaking arrangements for the following day. The moment I stepped over the threshold I knew that I had accepted my mother's death; not just in that I did not expect her greeting at the door or for her to be moving about in all the old familiar routines, but at a different level as well.

Since neither Bob nor I nor Candace felt much like sleeping, we stayed up and talked, trying to clear away some of the horror and relieve Candace of some of the burden.

Everyone was very helpful. The women of the Church brought over loads of food—all kinds of casseroles, meats, salads, and desserts. They started arriving Sunday and were still going strong when we left. It is really a very good idea since one must eat something and yet one never feels like preparing a meal.

The funeral was held at Holy Trinity Church at two o'clock. It is a charming, dark-framed church with a faintly old-fashioned air to it. Dad and I had gone over earlier for a celebration of the Holy Communion. I felt very strongly that if I could receive our Lord, I should find what lay ahead easier to bear.

I had never heard the Burial service read before. I hadn't even read it myself, so I did not know what to expect. But later I had occasion to thank God for the wisdom, restraint, and dignity of the Burial service, as of all other services in the Prayer Book. The only other funeral I had ever attended before was, by contrast, barbarous and uncivilized.

It was somewhat amusing to Candace and me to step into the monstrous limousine sent over by the mortuary. (In my naiveté I had assumed that we would simply drive over to the church or go with friends!) It was black, with powder blue upholstery, air vents as on an airplane, and other unexpected technological details. I don't understand why such elegant comfort is thought to be desirable at such a time, unless, perhaps, to distract one's attention—as it did mine. Further comic relief was provided by the liveried escort-chauffeur whose mien and oily unctuousness I simply did not know existed outside of Dickens. We were told when and where to step, what to do in every particular—even when it was abundantly clear. If I were not supposed to be able to see or hear or take a step in any direction without falling on my face, then perhaps I was doing better than I thought I was.

As for flowers, I remember being slightly surprised that the "spread" Bob and I and Dad and Candace had provided was merely a band of flowers. But it was attractive: carnations, mums in bronze tones, and yellow roses. I cannot recall any of the others; certainly there weren't many, because we had requested people to make, instead, a contribution to the local Mental Health Fund. (I heartily agree with the growing body of opinion that a funeral should be kept as simple and as inexpensive as possible. I feel that a Requiem Eucharist, for example, is a far better act of remembrance than any kind of material display. So much of the time people are prompted by public sentiment and pressured by social custom to put far more into a funeral than can possibly be afforded. If one wants to, and can manage it without depriving others, there are far more serviceable memorials than elaborate floral wreaths and headstones: gifts to the Church, to medical research programs, or to some public or educational institution. I even wonder if such concern with the physical body is consistent with a Christian view of death and burial.)

Nearly a hundred people had already gathered at the church: all neighbors and friends, but no relatives except ourselves. (The only other relative in the immediate vicinity,

Aunt Margaret, was away at the time.) After we arrived the coffin was wheeled in, closed and draped, and the service began.

As it proceeded down the aisle I felt as if I were being forced down into the deepest core of reality. I was meeting, at long last, the very thing I had dreaded but so far evaded. I expected to disintegrate utterly, to be so wounded within as to be forever after emotionally crippled and mentally deranged. With bowed head, trembling knees, and complete relinquishment into God's hands I awaited the blow. Instead, strength seemed to arise in me like sap in a tree. I was lifted up into a Power that was beyond all knowing or believing. Incredibly, joy overwhelmed me—not the joy I had known before in God, the joy that comes on quickly, as though running footsteps were bringing delight, but a feeling more like the fierce, struggling, and conquering joy that a woman experiences in childbirth. To my utter amazement I was experiencing God as the Father. I had before experienced God as Christ, and many times as the indwelling Holy Spirit, but never before God the Father Almighty. I had known there was a Father, or more accurately, I believed on faith that there was, but I had never had any firsthand knowledge of Him. My sorrow was swallowed up in awe and love. And the Psalmist's declarations were made:

> God is our hope and strength, a very present help in trouble. Therefore will we not fear, though the earth be moved, and though the hills be carried into the midst of the sea. . . .

> The sorrows of death compassed me. . . .

> For thou, O God, hast proved us; thou also hast tried us, like as silver is tried.

Thy way is in the sea, and thy paths in the great waters, and thy footsteps are not known.

Thou shalt not be afraid for any terror by night, nor for the arrow that flieth by day. . . .

O God, my heart is ready. . . .[1]

Before, I could appreciate such lines, both as a poet and out of my own human experience, but never understandingly. One wants to shout, "Yes! . . . Yes! . . . Of course! . . . How could it be otherwise?"

I was able to receive more of God this time. Before, I was blinded and afraid. Now there was more of me hollowed out, but not enough—never enough. "Flesh and blood cannot inherit the kingdom of God,"[2] nor can man in his mortality ever receive more than a particle of God. Yet God is so abundant, so shattering, that one's life is changed—changed in every aspect, so that never again can one be the same. This knowledge, this experience of God, is worth all that we have or ever can get. Anyone who has ever once been overshadowed by God promptly develops an insatiable need of Him, and to please Him nothing costs too much.

"In the twinkling of an eye"[3] is an apt phrase, and when I heard it I understood other things. I was at last able to believe, without the slightest reservation, in eternal life. I had believed in God before because I had known and loved Him, but about life to come I was far less certain. I predicated it, let us say, on the basis of what I knew of Christ, but now that time was flattened and disappeared, life had continuity, and I could see eternity.

Thus in her death Mother left all of us gifts: the gift of growth, the gift of love, the gift of God, and the gift of life.

I saw, too, that sorrow and love are inseparable. It is not

possible to have the one without the other. If you love, you are a hostage to life; and one is in proportion to the other. I never loved my mother more dearly than in that moment when I became willing to accept the entire measure of my sorrow in her death. I have never in my life been more fully involved in anything so wounding and shocking but, as the pain of childbirth is lessened by not tensing against it, so is the impact of grief lessened by yielding to it. It is not in escaping what is feared that one finds asylum, but in meeting it.

There had always been one part of Christ's life in which I had not been able to participate, and that was the Crucifixion. I could never understand how Christians could accept it, let alone glory in anything so unbelievably cruel and unnecessary. Could not man's salvation have been worked out some other way? If not, then let man die, and the sooner the better. Such was my attitude toward Christ's sacrifice on the cross. I dreaded Lent. On Good Friday it was all I could do to drag myself to church, and I ran back into the bright sunshine as soon as it was decently possible. I was all but renouncing Him and His gifts. I wanted Christmas and Easter without the dark stain of that terrible Day in between. But that is impossible, as I now see clearly. We can, I also see, learn all we need to know about God's purposes from the raw material of our own lives.

No doubt all this will be obvious to you, Lynn, having lost your father so recently. It was evident to me before, metaphysically. At twenty-two I could proclaim such things in poetry. But at the level at which truth can be acted upon, I had not understood it.

So—in that brief time, in that candlelit church, kneeling near my mother's body—God taught me, upheld me, and blessed me.

Later in the quiet and lovely San Gabriel cemetery, leaf-dappled, steeped in the fragrance of flowers and bird song, the ceremony was consummated.

But all is not over. There is Stan and what has to be done about him. There may be the publicity and suffering of a court trial. We shall all cry again, alone and bereft, every day the widening circles of our loss will reach out farther, memories of the past will surface and reach new planes of awareness. But I know now that we are grieving for ourselves; that our sorrow moves within the narrow structure of our lives, our habits, our associations, our dependencies.

All the days since have been lived with joyful concern for the needs of others and that speaks eloquently of the Kingdom of God. I've found that whenever stress or joy brings me closer to God I can in all my affairs move under the face of eternity, and I regret that I cannot live in this boundless way all the time.

In the midst of all the crowding concerns I shall never be able to forget that my mother stands closer to a brilliance that I myself cannot now bear, and I shall envy her a little for standing so much closer to the Source of that light.

While we were away, the children stayed with Fifi and Sven Dorf, some friends of ours. It was a reassuring place for them to be—out in the country with horses and dogs and the mountains, where they could do old-fashioned and comforting things like making popcorn balls and taffy, climbing trees, and feeding the animals. We always underestimate a child's involvement in a bereavement. Of course, Mark (still only four), apart from being unnerved by the air of strain around him, was relatively untouched, but Meredith was disturbed, and I hope I can soon give her the time and cuddling she needs.

However, I have discovered over and over again that we cannot (and probably should not even try to) protect children from the ultimate realities of life. They can sustain an unbelievable amount of pressure so long as they are firmly founded in love. To attempt to conceal, fabricate, minimize, mollify, or pervert the truth, is to do them a disservice. On an unconscious level children have probably grasped the situation anyway, and when we try to camouflage what cannot be hidden we end up by making them more uneasy and frightened. When and how are they to deal with the raw materials of life if we deny them any contact with such things until they are "old enough to understand"?

I hope that I have told you what you wanted to know—on the basis of what you said, and what I felt that I should want to know in your place. Knowing how much all of you loved Mother, I was hesitant about writing in such detail until I learned that Dad had already prepared you. And, as Candace says, it's something that doesn't make sense unless you know all of it.

I will keep in touch. Write to me when you can.

IX

Letter to Bob

Dearest Bob:

I started to write this letter to you a year and a half ago when we were talking one night about that series of tornadoes in the South which took so many lives, and you exclaimed bitterly, "God must really love mankind to permit this!" Your remark put me thinking about the problem of evil and pain, but I couldn't get very far with it because I wasn't ready then. Now that I'm better prepared, it seems almost unnecessary to revive the matter. When St. Bernard was asked why one should love God, he answered quite simply, ". . . the reason for our loving God *is* God."[1]

For a person such as you, a skeptic and unbeliever, all such answers are inadequate because they beg the question by assuming too much. I don't mean to imply that one has to attempt to prove the existence of God before he can approach all that is not God. Indeed, if there were no God there would be no dilemma: it is only when we try to reconcile the fact of evil and pain with the fact of a loving and merciful God that we seem to run into difficulties.

This problem did not constitute any great obstacle between myself and belief. There were other doubts that tormented me, but by the time I got around to considering this question, I already had a working faith. It was no longer necessary for me to set up a rationale to deal with each and every question that plagued me in everyday affairs. I had a much more direct and, I felt, more reliable means of dealing with these matters—experience and faith.

Yet if someone had said to me, back in those early days, "Your experience and your faith in God will make all this clear to you eventually," it would have been, however true, a futile remark. The concept of faith as a source of information and insight, as well as a rule, had never occurred to me; by definition, it could not. At that time I thought of faith as something rather static and self-limiting, a convenient repository for all unanswerable questions, unmanageable doubts. I scorned the leap of faith where the mind, unable to go further, fell into the arms of the Church. About that time I read, I remember, the account of Raissa Maritain's search for God; it impressed me as a vigorous and honest inquiry—much along the path I wanted to think I was taking—a perceptive and incisive questing by a mind not afraid to put God to the test of spirit and intelligence. So I was dumbfounded when her faith capitulated into something I could not understand. I felt disappointed and cheated; I felt she had given up, when actually she had given in. I was still a long way from such a surrender.

From where I stand now I can look both forward and backward. I am not far enough away from my own doubts not to be able to appreciate yours. (Indeed, I hope I'll never reach the point where I will not be able to respect a man's honest reservations!) At the same time I can see that Christianity is an experimental religion. Each person finds something a little different in it and each one gives back something of his own to it. St. Paul was aware of this. So, each must find his own way—by testing, by backtracking, by trying again and again, by leaning his weight first on this side and then on the other. It is rather like a blind man trying to thread a needle.

You will not like this. You would rather have an infallible guide, with every turn marked clearly. You say that unless every word of the Bible has been personally dictated by God it has no validity. Like St. Thomas, unless you see the Risen Christ with your own eyes, you cannot believe. But anyone who charts his own course comes to the conviction of truth that is not possible outside of experience. I know that rough and homely dealing with reality combined with an honest search for God does produce faith, which, in the end, is the perception of hidden truth. Does the poet have a different kind of truth from the scientist? Can we say that either is less true than the other?

What I propose to do here will not in any way be exhaustive, and will leave unanswered many aspects of the question which the theologian, the historian, the scientist would consider important. If I were writing a book on religion, systematically organized by subject matter, I might undertake to do it, but like most writers who attempt to deal with matters beyond their ken I would fail. Even in this simple letter I may not succeed, but at least I will have a better chance if I confine myself to those aspects of the problem of evil and pain that I have been concerned with personally.

I've been talking about faith, and the first question that comes to mind is: How can we possibly have faith unless we have free will? If God gave us no choice but belief, there would be no need for faith. But, given free will, how can evil be avoided? To me, this is the crux of the whole matter and I will come back to it from time to time. But before we can have any understanding of this we have to approach the question from different vantage points, considering different kinds of evil. Not all evil is moral, although we sometimes act as if it were.

First of all, is there evil in nature? It seems to me that there are certain inherent operations in nature which seem to us so absolute, so independent of us, that we are tempted to call them "laws" of nature, although the physicist warns us against being too dogmatic about this. One thing, however, is certain: they are not arbitrary—they do not operate for the benefit of, or at the will of, one man at one time and another man at another time.

In his book *The Problem of Pain*, C. S. Lewis says:

> Again, if matter has a fixed nature and obeys constant laws, not all states of matter will be equally agreeable to the wishes of a given soul, nor all equally beneficial for that particular aggregate of matter which he calls his body. If fire comforts that body at a certain distance, it will destroy it when the distance is reduced. . . . If a man travelling in one direction is having a journey down hill, a man going in the opposite direction must be going up hill. . . . In a game of chess you can make certain arbitrary concessions to your opponent, which stand to the ordinary rules of the game as miracles stand to the laws of nature. You can deprive yourself of a castle, or allow the other man sometimes to take back a move made inadvertently. But if you conceded everything that at any moment happened to suit him—if all his moves were revocable and if all your pieces disappeared whenever their position on the board was not to his liking—then you could not have a game at all. So it is with the life of souls in a world: fixed laws, consequences unfolding by causal necessity, the whole natural order, are at once the limits within which their common life is confined and also the sole condition under which any such life is possible. Try to exclude the possibility

of suffering which the order of nature and the existence of free-wills involve, and you find that you have excluded life itself.[*2]

Isn't pain in some sense a physical necessity? What would we do without it? For example, when we examine a case of "syringomyelia" (where the nerves do not carry pain-bearing messages to the brain and the patient therefore has no pain sensations whatever), we see how pathetic and dangerous life is for anyone who has no pain to warn him of injury or illness. *Any disassociation from reality, whether from physical or psychological pain, brings about a state of disease or morbidity in an organism. It is not in the pain, but in the escape from it, that the threat to our security lies.*

How could God intervene at every point to circumvent pain and evil and at the same time allow cause and effect, free will, gestation, life itself? Tornadoes, accidents, disease—all extraneous disasters that seem to strike us indifferently—are just as much a part of man's experience as the unexpected blessings, the "close calls," the danger averted, the life saved. Sometimes we thank God for the good, but blame Him for the evil as though we, attempting to mastermind creation, were imputing to nature a free will of its own.

There are some things God cannot do, and one of them is

---

* I must disagree with C. S. Lewis on his definition of miracles as exceptions to the laws of nature like the *j'adoube* maneuver in the chess game. They seem to be exceptions, but are they really? Perhaps there is more inherent in nature than we can guess. There was a time when an atomic explosion would have been classed in the realm of the miraculous. But atoms, molecules, electrons—they were there all the time; man had only to find them and learn how to combine them properly to trigger the fission. This is not to deny miracle, but to suggest that it may not operate in the way we think it must; that is, by the abrogation or suspension of a "law" of nature.

to give us free will and at the same time withhold that freedom from us. One need not be a Christian to be thoroughly convinced that man brings all manner of evil upon himself: suffering, sorrow, worry, cruelty, fear—the list is endless. The more we learn about man, the more we see his inhumanity to his own kind. Psychosomatic medicine has added disease, both functional and organic, to the variety of ills man inflicts upon himself, sometimes unconsciously but nevertheless actually. It is curious to note that those who have separated themselves farthest from God are those who suffer the greatest anxiety, whatever form it may take. We all know the crabbed, querulous pessimist, the emotionally cold—those who exhibit what William James calls the "pining puling mumping mood," so destructive to ourselves and others. I've never found that among Christians. I'm not talking about the "Sunday Christians," but those who are dwelled in by God and who participate in a fuller response toward Him and all men. They, too, are victims of tornadoes, accidents, disasters; but, because they have so little of the inner cancer which eats away at others, they have reserves sufficient not only for themselves but for others.

Many people believe, and not without reason, that apart from man's own machinations, there is such a thing as external evil. Whether we personify it as Satan or call it merely a contrary force at work in the universe, it certainly does seem to be operative. If we look at our own experience thoughtfully we will see that we do indeed meet it in the recalcitrance of nature, in temptation, and in the deflection of our desire to do good; and we are content to characterize it vaguely as a form of constraint laid upon everybody. But not until we seriously undertake to do God's will does it appear to be something personal. Our Lord speaks of the Devil. The testimony of the saints amounts almost to a detailed study of his craft. So far, I myself know very little of the Adversary, or even if such a being exists; it may be that I have not gone far enough in the service of God to warrant the Devil's attention! However that may be, serious-minded and sophisticated people quite seriously attest to his hampering and demoralizing activities.

But this I know: the more I know of good the more I learn of evil.* There was a time, and not many years ago, when I was highly amoral. I tried not to hurt others, and if my intentions were sound that was all that really mattered. The concept of sin was to me picturesque and archaic. After I joined the Church my early self-examinations had largely to do with fringe faults, stepping circumspectly around the poisonous miasma of my own rottenness. Impatient to behave as a Christian, I tried to acquire virtue only to find that one cannot begin to know of what it consists until he moves closer to God. Only as our pitiful lives are thrown up against that of Christ can we commence to have any hint of the depths of evil within us.

In any discussion of evil and pain we should not lose sight of the fact that God was not made for man, but man made for God. Those of us who have been nurtured in a humanist philosophy find this difficult to reckon with. If the

---

* St. Augustine insists that we cannot know evil apart from good. However, I'm not sure that I can go all the way with him in his argument that evil is the "privation of good," having no existence in itself. I tend to be wary of any attempts to identify evil with non-being, because of the implicit temptation to deny evil—and this should be avoided at all cost. If evil can exist, if it can be real, purposive, regulative, and causative and still be in the realm of non-being, then I would have to agree with St. Augustine. This is no doubt a semantic difficulty, because I have to admit that total evil is total lack of the presence of God.

universe were man-centered the very thought that anything could occur in his domain that would be contrary to his presumed good would, indeed, be intolerable. But whether or not we believe it, whether or not we like it, God has fashioned our world and ourselves, and in Him we move and have our being.

God did not even spare His only-begotten Son and yet, oddly enough, we expect God to spare us. Do we seriously think that the Man who was "despised and rejected . . . a man of sorrows, and acquainted with grief"[3] took the cross upon His shoulders in order to ease the way for us?

· Nowhere does the word "happiness" appear in the Authorized Version of the Bible; "pleasure," "joy," "blessing" abound, but never the sort of enduring, contented felicity that "happiness" connotes. Modern man has come to consider happiness his due portion in life, but he forgets that God never promised it to him. "He said not: thou shalt not be troubled; thou shalt not be tempted; thou shalt not be distressed. But He said: thou shalt not be overcome."[4]

Still, comfort is important to us, and happiness inevitably becomes the final good. At every turn our society aids and abets us in our flight from reality. Whenever we are in danger of coming to grips with the facts, the practised arts of escape and self-deception are applied. The copy writer dispels the suspicion that we may be aging, that our lives or our homes may be ugly and decaying. The crooner lulls us into thinking that we may be alone, shipwrecked on an island of our own selfish isolation. The politician assures us that the status quo —whatever that is—should be maintained. The psychiatrist convinces us that we are victims of our environment. The teacher tells us what we want to hear about our children. The physician promises us that we will recover from our illness.

The clergyman sentimentalizes our religion so much that we expect little from it and give little back to it, so that the Church appears to be a social institution—something designed to "uplift" us and encourage fellowship and "togetherness."

But, like Job, we ourselves are blameless. We sit under the banana tree, as in the Steig cartoon, and contemplate our innocence. We say that we are not responsible for war, privation, murder. If we are not, why is it, then, that we feel so guilty? We'll find a scapegoat every time. Whenever we say of a man, "He would be better off dead," we really mean, "He bears the image of my hate, and in his death he will take some of my guilt with him." The greater our own involvement, the quicker our disclaimer.

Archibald MacLeish, in writing about his modern parallel to Job, observes, "Job is not answered in the Bible by the voice out of the whirling wind. He is silenced by it . . . by the might and majesty and magnificence of creation. He is brought, not to know, but to see. As we also have been brought."[5] Perhaps we can never know. But, if we are not blinded, we can see deeply and with fulfillment into the nature of evil and our own selves. The man who shakes his fist at God has not seen what is in his own hand.

There is justice in the universe, but not necessarily our kind of justice.

How many times does not good come out of evil? That is an imponderable question; it cannot be answered because we cannot, at the time, always see the good that accrues; much of the time we never see it. Often we are not ready to, at least not until our rebellion subsides.

I remember that last summer my mother and I were discussing this whole matter and that she startled me by asking, "Why did Nana have to die?" I had never known either why my grandmother "had to die," but suddenly I did know: it was so that I could have a mother.

My grandmother was not financially dependent on our family, but she had lived with us on and off throughout my childhood. She had a gay, outgoing, and attractive personality which, coupled with the tolerance and indulgence for which grandparents are notorious, led me to prefer her company to that of my mother, and to love her more dearly. When I was fourteen she died quite suddenly from pneumonia. Her death hit me hard, and coming as it did in the midst of the strains and stresses of my adolescence, I turned more and more to my mother. Before then I seldom saw my mother; she was always, it seemed, involved in academic pursuits. Now, without Nana to function as a sitter for us, a more normal family life was established and I came to know and love my mother; we were forced to find each other.

Perhaps there were other reasons, more important ones— I don't know. Reasons are what everyone seems to look for. Probably the first question asked after a great loss is the anguished, unanswered cry of "Why?"

The other day I looked at the wrong side of our daughter's embroidery hoop, an awkward and unlovely tangle of knots and unconnected patterns of thread, and was surprised, when I turned it over, at the beauty of the design. If I could not even picture the composition of the front by looking at the back of an artifact of an eight-year-old, I dare say that I am in no position to make pronouncements on the human dilemma from my side of the hoop! Chance and circumstance are too interwoven for the human mind to follow. Fortunately, however, we are not dependent upon our reason alone.

Until recently, every time I said the Lord's Prayer I had

qualms about the lines "Thy Kingdom come. Thy will be done, On earth as it is in heaven." It was all so unnerving because it implied a readiness to accept His will. For my part there had certainly been no full acquiescence. I had always added in my heart the provision, "If I can bear it"—suggesting, of course, that if I could not, I was not wholly asking that His will be done.

God brought that evasion to a halt some time ago when, in a crisis, He left me bereft of His help when I most desperately sought it. In despair, at the mercy of forces beyond me, and feeling utterly forsaken of God, I made a foolish, and what could have been dangerous, choice. Later I discovered that help would have come had I been able to hold on for one more hour! From this I learned that God expected me to take the responsibility for my own choices. He had supported me long enough. Now I was ready to take some steps on my own.

I learned further that while His grace would always be sufficient, it was not up to me to determine how much I was able to bear, or by what means or in what time help would be given. So it was that I was prepared to meet the crisis of my mother's death. Truly, "He delivers the afflicted by their affliction."[6]

I had wondered why I was being hurried along, pushed, prodded whenever I showed signs of apathy. I used to protest to God, and wondered that since I was such a mess when I came to Him, was it necessary to alter a lifetime of negligence at such breakneck speed? Couldn't I lie down with a laurel or two and catch my breath? Apparently not. Failure to have met this latest tragedy would not simply have ended in dereliction of duty and in remorse, but it would have seriously threatened my faith and ultimately my well-being. In the three years since

I began my search there is scarcely an area in my life that has not been altered; the changeover has not been easy.

The Disciples, too, had three years of preparation, and see what they set out to accomplish at the end of it! We are tempted to exclaim that they had special grace. But did they? True, they were rather simple men whose lives were transformed, but was not Christ in their midst? Do we have any less? I don't think so; I think we have more because we have the advantage of history and twenty centuries of a witnessing Church. Where two or three of us are gathered together there will He be in our midst.

I am always protesting that I am not ready. I cling to my newly-won status, loath to take any decisive step forward. I know that there are some things you have to do only once, and I know there will be other crises, other doubts, other losses in my life, but in meeting my mother's death in the full acceptance of God's will I know that, in a sense, I have met them all. Before, there was always the nagging doubt that while everything was all right now, what would happen when the chips were down? I was halfway convinced that if I were ever really pushed I would not only fall apart as a person but would lose my faith as well. Anyone who has not been tested in the white heat of God's love may well harbor such doubts. We are taught, and we are changed—to our own immeasurable advantage. The classic question, "Why, if God loves us, does He permit such things to happen?" might very well be answered, *"Because* He loves us."

To resist the will of God is to spoil it, even though that will is a taking away. This idea is not, as I had once supposed, a sop to sorrow. It is not enough to say that the will of God shall prevail and it is useless to fight it. The sort of resignation that Goethe ended up with was a barren thing compared with what the Christian finds in acceptance, in the vital giving of our wills back to God. A covenant has been made, an exchange has been effected. That is what we do in the Eucharist at the words: "And here we offer and present unto thee, O Lord, our selves, our souls and bodies, to be a reasonable, holy, and living sacrifice unto thee. . . . " Whenever we make our communion, we receive Him. Yet it is never an act of God only. We say that we "partake" of our Lord's Body and Blood, but that is not entirely complete: we must give something in return—whether it be the full offering of ourselves or merely the setting aside of our selfish desires.

Many times now I have noticed the astonishing results of such a spiritual transaction. I used to think that the grace was to be found in taking a decisive step of some sort, but in looking back I see that in each case it lay in some sacrifice on my part: with God's help there was a letting go of some part of myself that I once considered necessary to my life. With me it had been a niggardly proffering; I had wanted to hold something back. Left to my own devices I am sure I would never have been able to achieve any complete surrender. No doubt those with less stubborn natures can discover all this with less shock, but it can never be an agreeable undertaking, for otherwise there would be no sacrifice. Unless we stand to lose something, we have given nothing. And it must be a total letting go; we must see it as a *fait accompli*, and accept it as such, much as Abraham did with the sacrifice of his son Isaac—it was then, and not before, that God could give him the fruits of obedience.

In my case offerings have always been accompanied by a Pentecostal joy: somehow I never expect it and it always takes me by surprise. But this is only because I have been learning how to give and, as I have said before, God is very patient and gracious with beginners. I must be careful to avoid thinking of my newly found joy in terms of a reward or anything due me. I expect that, now a full submission has been made, I shall have to learn how to make it in all kinds of spiritual weather. The sun will not always shine. This is as it should be: the very hardiness of our souls depends upon a rigorous climate. How else, for those of us who are not saintly, can we be sufficiently stimulated to put down our roots at all?

Again and again I have found how vitally necessary it is for us to make the choice, to open ourselves on the Godward side. His response to us, His revelation to us is contingent upon our readiness to receive Him. I so often hear you say that if there really were a God, He should be willing to show Himself to us, that we might know without a doubt what He is, where He is, and what He wants us to do. I once thought so, too. But you cannot know God without seeing how impossible all this is. Again, He cannot both give us free will and at the same time withhold it. In our behalf He will safeguard our freedom of choice by refusing to coerce, to impinge upon, to compel, our loyalty. He does not command; He invites. Jesus Christ showed us this when He looked down from the mountain of temptation and saw the alternative, a *deus ex machina* who would abundantly supply man's needs and force his belief by a demonstration of miracle and power. In His choosing Christ revealed to us the nature of God.

Furthermore, to suppose that we, as we are, might see God fully is unthinkable. The conviction of the Hebrews that to look upon God was to die was not so much superstition. When the author of Hebrews tells us that "It is a fearful thing to fall into the hands of the living God,"[7] he does so advisedly. Wherever sinful man encounters his Creator he must back away expeditiously. But in the full presence of God could he do that—back away? This is no mere speculation. Consider the saints who, through a lifetime of love, have been capable of receiving such a largesse of Him fearlessly and ecstatically. It is the same God, the fire of whose countenance can both disfigure and transfigure. We do not know what we ask.

This, in my way of thinking, is the best support for the idea of purgatory. There is very little clear Scriptural evidence for it, yet we know that few of us at our death are prepared to receive God fully. The only good sense is to presume that we have to grow—to "go from strength to strength," until we *can* reach God in His glory.

But in this life is there no other way for us to grow except by what we call "negative values"? Moreover, is there any way by which pain, disease, and death can be considered universal "givens"? Or do they operate capriciously, at random, in an arbitrary way? At the beginning of this letter, I referred to C. S. Lewis on the matter of causal necessity, and showed that the physical laws of the universe can operate in one man's favor and at the same time to another man's detriment. If a summer storm waters and nourishes one farmer's fields it may drown another man's crops. There is also the "if this, then that" relationship that is inviolable, as in the law of gravity. Can we find anything similar in the moral sphere?

Much as we loathe to admit it, I am afraid that we can. We constantly try to circumvent what is known as "natural law," to deny that there is something inflexible about the consequences of our behavior, to deny any relationship between what we sow and what we reap. We need not have any religious feelings to be able to see that there are some things which no man, at any time or in any circumstance, can do without violating himself.

There is a universal moral law, as distinct from a moral code, which consists of certain statements of fact about the nature of man; and by behaving in conformity with which, man enjoys his true freedom. . . . The more closely the moral code agrees with the natural law, the more it makes for freedom in human behavior; the more widely it departs from the natural law, the more it tends to enslave mankind and to produce the catastrophes called "judgments of God."[8]

Moral laws, like the laws of nature, are discoverable by experience. The man who is consistently irritable, ungracious, or irascible will inevitably find himself rejected and disliked. It would seem that there is at least some agreeableness required for admission into any fellowship. Consider the disruption and disorientation of a broken home, the violence that breeds violence, the neglect of the body that invites disease, the torment of the undisciplined mind, the depression that begets despair, the sins of the fathers visited upon the sons. The man who persistently injures others must, sooner or later, harm himself. If he escapes the penalty of the civil law he has yet to deal with his own conscience; if he escapes that, he may face the repudiation of his fellows and subsequent loneliness; if he escapes that, he still has to contend with himself, when, committed to his own custody, he is imprisoned in that ultimate hell where a person is ignorant of his own evil. According to von Hügel the characteristic of lost souls is "their rejection of everything that is not simply themselves."[9]

We do not need to be omniscient (although that would help!) to see the ruin that is the unavoidable consequence of wrong choices. Nowhere is it more obvious or more dramatic than in the case of the alcoholic who, quite simply, has three choices: reformation, insanity, or death. The alcoholic learns at first hand, the hard way, through his own experience, the operations of natural law. The disease can indeed be arrested by the will; but the alcoholic eventually discovers that he cannot make much headway on his own but must, for his own salvation, reckon with the will of God. If there are no atheists in foxholes, it may be said that there are no unbelievers among former alcoholics who have recovered sobriety.

But good—like evil—is often not this simple. Actually it is, but we cannot usually see it: to us it remains mixed and complex and relative. I suspect it is that way because we want it that way; by clouding the issue we can, for the time being at least, avoid doing what is difficult and repugnant to us. For those of us who are ready to do the will of God it is comparatively simple, especially for those who are willing to take Him at His word.

I had always supposed that the vows taken by members of Religious Orders were somehow arbitrarily made, that there were other vows that could just as well lead to a proper relationship with God. Now I begin to see that there is something necessary in obedience, poverty, and chastity, that self-sacrifice itself brings out the best within us. I myself have always wanted to compromise; I have reasoned that it was not always possible to obey Christ's admonition to sell all that we had, give it to the poor, and take up the cross and follow Him. (Who, then, would be the poor?) I had wanted to believe that while "power tends to corrupt; and absolute power corrupts absolutely"[10] a little bit of power, judiciously used, could be of value.

Obviously a compromise is possible: we make it every day, but to the extent we make it, we will fall short of what we expect of ourselves—and what God expects of us. Unfortunately, most of us are not interested either way, and so we cannot very well know what our capacities really are. We are not prepared for what C. S. Lewis calls "the intolerable compliment" God has paid us by loving us. We become so dependent upon material possessions, upon the possession of each other, and upon what we like to call self-reliance, that the very thought of relinquishing our own desperate hold is unthinkable. But the experience and testimony of those who have let go—the Franciscans, for example—show us that they have attained what we have been striving for: security and love; but they found it another way.

If there were any easier way I, for all my laziness, would have found it. A way less fearful, less arduous, less demanding —isn't that what most of us look for? Yet no one has found such a way. If pain and death were not needed to show forth love, why, then, is the cross necessary? And why is it that only those who are able "naked to bear the naked cross"[11] find the greatest truth, the fullest life, and the largest measure of love?

If there were no God there would be, of course, other ways; without a God-centered universe we could justifiably take pleasure only in ourselves, rely solely upon our own efforts, and concern ourselves with the demands of our moment-to-moment existence. To ask if all this would be easier or better is at best an unfruitful question. To those who have struggled to find a substitute for God, or to those who have known and experienced Him, the thought of a Godless universe is laughable. Anyone who really wants to, can find it out for himself. I used to wonder, when Bishop Lewis would speak of ultimate Reality as that which we would have to reckon with eventually, what was so compelling about it, especially for the unbeliever. It is, I am beginning to see, the sum and substance of things-as-they-are.

For me as an artist there is one further argument for the

necessity of evil and pain. When people say, "This is too good to be true" they are not only acknowledging an accepted fact about human experience—that it is rarely compounded of pure pleasure—but also recognizing their instinctive need for an admixture of good and evil. We do not think much of a writer who is content with a banal description of nothing but pleasant events. We protest, "Life isn't like that," meaning not only that this isn't an accurate account of the way things stand, but that it falls short of greatness. In art we do not seek the trivial, but the difficult: the dilemma resolved, the puzzle solved, the impediment overcome. Man's nobility emerges only in the struggle. Art convinces us, if life has not, that affirmation is stronger after doubt, pleasure the more poignant after pain, courage possible only after fear. Moreover, we recognize, as Milton did, that evil can often become our good, thricefold and sanctified.

Isn't this what art is really about? We are never content until we can evoke a broken, fragmentary glory. Beauty always makes and mars; it is a fit mooring for the fey and fallow heart. We would not have it otherwise. The hero in a play becomes articulate only when he despairs of utterance. A dancer's grace grows out of the subduing of the hostile forces of gravity and the limitations of the human body. A tonic chord in music can bring resolution only after the brooding discord. And so in painting where depth is achieved only through the vital contrast of light and shadow. Now would we truly want all mystery to be laid bare to sight? It would seem that if we should ever lose the bitter with the sweet, it would be better that man should never be complete.

Here I am speaking only of man in his mortality. Those who ask about eternal life, "What will we have to strive for?" do not consider how marvelously God provides for man's needs. (Any state of existence without God would be at the very best dull. The idea of survival merely for survival's sake is abhorrent.) I believe that absolute happiness, like God Himself, can be borne only after a change has been wrought in us. Until then it would appear that, like the pearl dependent upon the grain of sand in the oyster, our growth is dependent upon the grit of sin, the friction of pain, the stress of evil.

From all of this can we justifiably draw any conclusions about the nature of God? I don't see why we can't, if, of course, we are aware of the limitations of our own understanding. Nicolas Berdyaev claims, it seems to me quite accurately, that "In the case of man, that which he creates is more expressive of him than that which he begets. The image of the artist and the poet is imprinted more clearly on his works than on his children."[12] We can learn something about God the Creator by observing His creation. St. Thomas Aquinas maintains that we cannot say anything significant about God without recourse to analogy. This is what I meant earlier when I talked about the truth of the poet. Dorothy Sayers takes us one step further in her book, *The Mind of the Maker,* in which she makes a strong case for a parallel between the divine and the artistic imagination.

Now let us take another step and see what happens. Oscar Wilde has said, not without irony, that life imitates art. I believe that there is a good deal of truth in his statement: it is in art that we find archetypes of behavior, rare insights into the nature of things, and intimations of immortality. I should like to use the same idea, but apply it to good and evil. Can we who are made in the image of God conceive of a great work of art in which all stress, suffering, shadow, deprivation, or discord is totally lacking? Can we, similarly, imagine a speck of creation without any of those elements? Not only would it lack the master touch, but it would be a void—negative, inactive, incapable of germination, unfitted for anything.

I am not speaking now of man's estate before the Fall, for at least the possibility of evil had to be present if free will were to be guaranteed, but I am saying that any speculation about man, either before his birth as natural man or after his death, is bound to be futile. At both points a change occurs: in the first instance, a change from, in the second, a change to, something that is beyond the scope of our knowledge. Somewhat like the unborn infant, alive in its darkness, and divided from the light of the world by the placental barrier, we know little about the life into which we shall be born; indeed, there is little that we can know. But as the fetus bears the stamp of its mortality, we—through Christ's all-begetting sacrifice—bear the mark of our immortality. I am speaking now of creation as we know it and of man as we know him. In both, it is clear that all the elements of pain, sorrow, disease, and death necessarily had to be present for man's restoration. Our Lord, in assuming our humanity, would not have it otherwise—for that was exactly the will of the Father.

Evil, pain, sorrow, and all the rest are here, not as meaningless obstructions, not as useless restraints, not as swords of destruction, but as implements of our salvation. The impingement of evil upon our lives is permitted by a God who loves us enough to risk our rebellion. Even we, despite what we know and feel and want, will ignore immediate danger and present discomfort in order to secure something better for ourselves and our children. How much more will our heavenly Father do for us!

Here I must return, where I began, to God Himself. If we would understand or appreciate a work of art, it is not enough to read an æsthetic analysis of it. When I first heard Brahms' *German Requiem* I was so delighted with it that for nearly a year I listened to it without "program notes." Later, when I read them, I learned which psalms and passages of Scripture were included, learned something about Brahms' life during this period, and read a critique of the work. It was interesting and enlightening, but it added nothing to the essential "truth" or the values I had already enjoyed. Had I known nothing about music such details perhaps would have helped me to appreciate it. But we reach a point in our musical life where such information is not only unnecessary but often a hindrance to our fullest enjoyment. For the person who is ready to listen, a piece of music can speak for itself.

So it is in our search for God. There comes a time when we are no longer content to learn about Him metaphysically, but must come to know Him personally. Then, at that point, all our questions, our doubts, our theological concerns become increasingly irrelevant. Men of all times, of all races, creeds, and colors, men of all places and stations differ in their ways of approaching God, but when the approach is that of experience, all agree that the encounter is unspeakable.

X

Letter to Sven

Reno, Nevada
August 10, 1959

Dear Sven:

Our conversation last night was such fun. Now that I am well on the way to forming religious convictions of my own, I need people like you to keep me alert, to force me to re-examine my own position. Church members need the stimulus and the challenge which the mind of a probing skeptic can provide. It is one thing to be satisfied with our faith but quite another to be complacent about it, as the convert is most keenly aware. Moreover, you made me see that we, as a body, are not giving you the insights you need; now I understand more clearly our failures and weaknesses as members of Christ's Body.

You say that you would like my comments on all the objections you raised, on the obstacles which will not allow you to return to the Church. I haven't gone far enough myself yet to speak firmly about any of it, for I have only three and a half years of Christian experience behind me. But our searches have been so similar that I can appreciate your reservations; after all, they were mine, too, not long ago.

I was glad to hear you say that you feel you must come to some conclusions about the nature of reality. That and the alacrity with which you approach the subject of religion

show a very real concern on your part. "Unconcerned detachment in matters of religion (if it is more than a methodologi-
cal self-restriction) implies an a priori rejection of the religious
demand to be ultimately concerned. It denies the object which
it is supposed to study objectively."[1] Or, as Father Cochrane
would put it, "It's all right to have an open mind, as long as
it is not open at both ends!"

As I understand it, you are coming to favor Buddhism
because of its "greater practicability" and the faith that its
philosophy generates "in the potential of man." (Here you
meant, I believe, the potential of the individual, not of mankind.) This really astonished me because I have found Christianity to have an abundance of both elements. I am assuming,
of course, that by "practicability" you mean something that
operates in our natural, daily lives; and by "the potential of
man," something that serves his highest good. Christianity,
as compared with the Eastern religions, is quite materialistic
and naturalistic. Christ came to minister unto man where he
(man) stood—limited in his senses, hedged about by physical
needs, laboring with the materials of this earth. All the Sacraments utilize commonplace, creaturely elements—bread and
wine, water, and oil. All the parables are told in terms of
routine, pedestrian human experiences.

But the Son of Man also ministered unto man's other
needs, which are just as urgent as having our daily bread, and
those are the needs you were talking and thinking about: a
restlessness and craving for something other than yourself, an
increasing sense of the inadequacy of your own life.

With maturity comes the wondering that perhaps one is
made for something else, that some purpose is not being fulfilled. I'm sure that at this point you would explain people's
failure in this respect by such things as financial deficiency,

sexual frustration, social privation, and lack of intellectual stimulation. Yet even when these problems are corrected, isn't there still a cry that will not be silenced? Wasn't it Carl Jung who found, among his own patients and those of his colleagues, that before the age of 35 most people's problems tend to center around sexual conflicts, and that after 35 they are largely religious concerns? In my own case, I never knew what I was thirsting for until I found God. It is in God that man finds his "potential"; it is in God that man sees his image—sees all that he can be and all that God wants him to be. This is the Christian's inheritance. Although we may never admit it, no matter how hard we try we can never quite forget it. It is this faculty which we express through music, the arts, delight in nature, and the love of others. Such expressions enrich our lives and the lives of others, but they can never quite spend the propulsive energy that thrusts up within us. It is what St. Augustine meant when he exclaimed, "For Thou hast made us for Thyself and our hearts are restless till they rest in Thee."[2]

But, you ask, aren't we left with a dichotomy—a conflict between this world and the next? We are indeed, and I don't see how a certain tension between the two can be avoided, just as there is some irreconcilable contention between the body and the spirit. We are so afraid of the word "tension": certain psychologists have done the world a great disservice by urging us to avoid tension at any cost; they would so dope us that we would be far too "tranquilized" to want, or even search for, a peace that passes understanding.

The truth remains, however, that we do exaggerate the conflict of body and spirit by compartmentalizing our spiritual life. That is why you get the impression that Christianity is exclusively an "other-worldly" cult: people enshrine their religion in a small, impoverished area of themselves, they confine their worship to Sundays and major feast days, they are so reverent of God—perhaps in a very sincere way—that they shrink from inviting Him into all the grubby little corners of their life. I suspect the reason why people do this, as I once did, and still find myself trying to do, is that we are lazy and we want to act independently of God. You see, we know that if we open ourselves to God we might have to lead Christian lives! It is far easier to relegate all that sort of thing to an easygoing Sunday morning affair.

All along the way we avoid being involved. Existentialism (whatever that is) has done at least one thing: it has stressed the necessity of involvement. That, I suspect, is why you are not finding satisfying answers through reason. I agree heartily with Archbishop Temple when he says, "The heart of Religion is not an opinion about God, such as Philosophy might reach at the conclusion of its argument; it is a personal relation with God."[3] And, I insist, that relationship is one that can and should be brought to bear upon every aspect of our lives. Nothing is so homely, insignificant, mundane, or unworthy that it cannot be reconciled to God through Him who said, "I am come that they might have life, and that they might have it more abundantly."[4] That is the idea of the whole Judeo-Christian tradition. That is exactly what the prophets were continually fighting for: religion in everyday life.*

So far we have, I believe, agreed, but I shall have to part company with you when you claim that corporate worship is not essential to religion. On the contrary, "The Church has to rediscover again and again its vocation, its *corporate voca-*

---

* Since I wrote this letter, a book has been brought to my attention which answers many questions about this whole matter: it is *Christian Belief and This World*, by Alec R. Vidler.[5]

tion as the witnessing community taken out of the world, *set apart* for God, but set apart in order to be again *sent* into the world."[6]

The "chosen people" of the Old Testament bore witness to the need of unity; those of the New Testament, to the need of fellowship. The early members of the Christian Church sustained each other and promoted the work of the Church by gathering together, by breaking bread, by sharing all things, by bearing each other's burdens. If Christianity had continued in this strong corporate union I imagine that man's subsequent history might have been different. How, for example, could Communism flourish? There would simply be no need for it.

You complain of the lack of Church unity, but might not that be the result of the very thing you are suggesting when you say that religion is something private, that we can worship God all by ourselves and in our own way? Instead of being what St. Paul called us—each a cell in the Mystical Body of Christ—we Christians are separated and divided, and consequently the power (which you find lacking in the Church) is, I agree, greatly diverted and wasted.

I do not believe that you can even, as you put it, "revere mankind" in isolation; much less can you worship God in such a manner. That is not to say that we shall not have our private prayers, that we shall not seek Him out on some mountain or by some lake; but our wilderness experiences are not enough to maintain our relationship to God. The very word "religion" is akin to the Latin verb "to bind"—it is meant to bind us to God through each other. I long ago discovered that I could not even sin *by myself* since, in every instance, a relationship of some kind was broken; nor can I progress alone, because I am dependent not only upon God, but also upon

172

many many others. Moreover, I am dependent upon the Church; much of the grace I receive comes to me through the Sacraments and the fellowship of other Christians who, through their own experience, help me to enrich my own. Having just returned from another two weeks at Camp Galilee, I am acutely aware of how much other people, in our group discussions and in their behavior, have influenced me and how, through them, God reveals Himself.

It seems to me that a person cannot be a good Christian without the Church any more than a man can be a good soldier without the Army. We need to be trained, and we need to be mobilized. If we try seriously to be Christians, we find ourselves engaged in warfare.

> We see a vision of the Christian life as it really is: a task for strong men, an obstinate and venturesome siege, a storming of an almost impregnable stronghold. As soon as a man really sets himself to follow Christ, he finds out that the Christian religion, so far from being namby-pamby, is a struggle, a conflict, a holy war, which calls forth all his powers of courage and fortitude and resolution.[7]

It is not, as you suppose, a religion for "nice" people. Your attitude is similar to the one I voiced in the first two letters of what now, it seems, may become a book. I, too, once viewed piety as an abomination, considered charity a weakness, and termed self-sacrifice needless. But as my understanding grows I am constantly astonished at the amount of courage and vigor that Christianity requires. It always demands more of us than we think we can give, but the miracle is that God is always pouring into us the strength that we can never acquire on our own.

That brings me to another one of your questions: what is

the difference between a Christian and a non-Christian? You said that there seems to be no significant difference between the two. Critical and aloof, I said the same thing, and I added, rather grandly, that if there were no difference, Christianity wasn't for me. At least in this I was correct, and you are, too; Christianity does, or should, make a difference in the life, behavior, and attitudes of anyone who is committed to it. But now that I have been "backstage," I know some very good reasons why a difference is not obvious to everyone.

In some people growth is slower than in others; the life that flows into us when we are grafted to Christ does not bear fruit instantly—sometimes not at all. Nor, when it does appear, is the fruit anything to rave about. You, perhaps—as I once did—look for something spectacular: something dramatic, phenomenal, and wondrous. You expect wonders of God, so it is natural that you would expect them of His children. But you are wrong there. Seldom does God overwhelm us with a prodigious display of His power. Rarely do His followers, even the saints, exhibit splendid signs of their indwelling God. God is not like that at all.

Consider how Christ was born—in a stable, among the beasts of the field. We sing,

> How silently, how silently,
> The wondrous gift is given!
> So God imparts to human hearts
> The blessings of his heaven.[8]

Remember that it was not until near the end of our Lord's earthly ministry that His Disciples, even after they had been with Him for nearly three years, became aware of His divine kinship with the Father. Even then many of them could not believe that He was the promised Messiah; after all, they had been awaiting a prince who would rule with pomp and glory. Isn't it true that we must first change ourselves in order to see the difference in others? Our blindness will not let us see what we are not prepared to find. When we are ready to see things as they really are—then it is Pentecost!

I have seen Christians living quiet, unobtrusive, and completely dedicated lives. I have seen them suffering without complaint, humbly accepting the will of God; their faith was no less than that of the martyrs who faced lions. I have often seen in others how acts of charity and self-sacrifice speak eloquently of the same faith. This is rare, of course, because Christ taught us to pursue our good works in secret; and those who live dedicated lives do just that. Those who are "hidden" in Christ often pass by unnoticed and unheard.

So far I have been speaking about totally committed Christians who, I will grant you, are not so many as we might wish but who are more numerous than we might suppose, simply because their holiness is not apparent. What about the rest of us, those who do not manage to keep that tension of which I spoke in proper balance, those who are not so fully dedicated? Some of us are not very likable as people, and we do things that offend others. With greater dedication much of this could be avoided, but not all. To be a Christian is not necessarily to be popular. Saying "no" to what everybody else does, not caring much about things by which the world sets great store, is bound to be unpopular. To be "a fool for Christ" is almost certain to win the appellation "odd ball"; almost always that "fool" meets with suspicion and hostility.

I had to learn something else. When I was new in the Church and came to be aware of God in an intimate way, and found such delight and joy in that relationship, I was arrogant enough to suppose that if others did not find the same thing they were missing the mark. Now I see that there are many ways in which we can respond to God—each affected, not only by our capacities, but also by our personalities. That is what St. Paul was trying to teach the members of the Church at Corinth.

Because this person or that does not respond to God or behave in what is your unique way, or in what is mine, need not mean that his service and worship are not as acceptable as ours. Indeed, his may be more acceptable, even though it seems to us lacking in fitness and propriety. Whenever I hear anyone refer to God as "my Buddy" or "my Podner" it sets my teeth on edge until I remind myself of something: when I was in Atlanta I had a Negro maid who kept telling me that "the Old Man upstairs" would pull her through. Having never heard this expression in reference to God, I was quite puzzled at first, and assumed she meant a solvent relative or, perhaps, a kind-hearted landlord!

You, for example, say, or imply, that virtue is a necessary hallmark of a Christian. But is it, really? Must we be *better* than others in order to qualify? If that is the case then the Gospel of Good News is very bad news! If I must be a righteous person in order to be a member of Christ, then I am most certainly lost, for then I'd have no need of Christ. But Jesus said that He came to call not the righteous, but sinners, to repentance. This is what salvation is all about; this is how we achieve an at-one-ment with God—not through our own efforts, but through Christ's sacrifice. We so take it for granted that we are in danger of forgetting that the cross is the basis of all Christian ethics. Christianity is Christ.

This is what the Holy Catholic Church so rightly emphasizes. To refer again to Suzanne de Dietrich:

Protestantism was born of Luther's reaction against a conception of salvation by works, and of his experience of justification by faith alone as the gospel's great message of reconciliation and deliverance. But there is a striking tendency in the history of Protestantism, especially Calvinist Protestantism, to revert in practice to the legalistic tendency of Judaism. It is the mark of legalism to lay stress on the law as a code of behavior, until law finally becomes a means of salvation, a substitute for the gospel. Where this happens, a new kind of pharisaism develops and the joy of salvation is lost. This joy of God which the Old Testament, at its best, already knew, will ring all through the apostolic proclamation. It is not among the Pharisees, but among the poor and humble of heart that "God made man" will choose his dwelling place. These are the true remnant, the Israel after God's heart, waiting for his Day.[9]

Still, you ask, isn't it true that a lot of people are Christians in name only? I'm sure they are, and I think it is because they do not really believe, they do not take God at His word, and consequently they are unable to become seriously involved in His plan of redemption. It has been said that a man does not genuinely believe that which he is not prepared to act upon. I think you are quite right in presuming that there must be some relation between belief and action.

Apart from our laziness and our unwillingness to take risks, there is something else: many of us simply do not know how far it is possible to go *with God's help*. We continually need to be converted, our faith needs to be revived in what we can do and dare. The majestic outpouring of God's grace is not limited to a favored few; it is the gift freely given to any who ask for it and will accept it. We are so handicapped by preconceived notions about the nature of God, we so repeatedly try to create Him in our own wobbly image, that it is no wonder we fail to hear His voice or feel His power. We want Him on our own terms, in our own time, and at our own convenience. More than that, few of us are prepared to forget ourselves long enough to search for God and His gifts. Happily for us, God is not proud; He will accept our most stunted offerings. Even by the slightest glance we can find Him at our side.

> Such knowledge is too wonderful and excellent
> for me; I cannot attain unto it.
> Whither shall I go then from thy Spirit? or
> whither shall I go then from thy presence?
> If I climb up into heaven, thou art there; if
> I go down to hell, thou art there also.[10]

The Psalmist speaks for all who have known God.

Elton Trueblood relates how Italian astronomers refused to look into the telescope to see the moons of Jupiter, whose existence Galileo claimed. Unenlightened, they felt secure in their stubborn conviction that they were right. "Truth is revealed in religion not just to anybody, but only to those who seek, and to those who *care*."[11] "Come and see" has been the universal invitation from the days when Andrew brought his doubting brother, Simon Peter. The test by experience is valid.

Yet countless numbers of Christians are without the full measure of their heritage. We have discussed the danger of reducing religion to a code of behavior, but it occurs to me that there is no less hazard in reducing religion to ceremonial observances—in allowing outward forms to do all the talking. This is apt to happen in our Church with all its symbolism and ritual and ceremonial. These things are valuable only so long as they remain in the category of means-to-an-end: a means to worship and holiness; but when they become, as they sometimes do, an end in themselves, we allow our whole faith to be put in jeopardy. We can hide behind words, music, emblems, devices, pageantry, and symbolic acts very easily, and before long we convince ourselves of our own devoutness and that we are engaged in all that God expects of us. It is just another form of Pharisaism. The very word I used— "just"—indicates how lightly we dismiss such practices. Pharisaism, above all else, was what our Lord found most repugnant. He gave the adulteress His blessing and forgave thieves and murderers, but He hurled His sternest denunciation at those who, in the eyes of the world, were above reproach. You are right in criticizing hypocrisy in the Church, but at the same time we must make sure that we ourselves are not also guilty of it. For example, I have sometimes caught myself taking a great deal of pleasure in a graceful genuflection, finding self-satisfaction in a letter-perfect recitation of the liturgy, or burnishing that halo you are always teasing me about! This is what happens when we make the practice of virtue its own reward.

I have left your pragmatic criticism until last. You say that if religion "works" it is a good sign of its validity; even more, that its validity is in proportion to its workability. I am afraid that I am rather uneasy about equating workability with truth. Fascism under Hitler certainly "worked" in that it succeeded in what it set out to do, but was it therefore necessarily true, right, or valid? This also makes truth all the more relative than even you, I think, would agree to; some things work under certain conditions and not under others, at one time and not another, for some people and not for others.

How, then, can a religion that purports to be universal accommodate so many contradictory elements?

Leaving aside all philosophical difficulties (I am sure you will find some obstacles here), let's consider this from a common-sense point of view. You say that if a religion offers people sizable rewards in terms of "comfort," "security," "ultimate answers," "peace of mind," and so forth, then the truth of that religion is enhanced. Here again I would have to agree with you—up to a point. Let me say right off that I am convinced that Christianity "works" far better than other religions, but not in the ways you have in mind. Comfort? Not if you are thinking of physical and spiritual ease. Security? Not if you have in mind immunity from the ills and hazards that beset all humankind. Ultimate answers? I have fewer answers now than I once thought I did! Peace of mind? Yes and no. Christians prefer to call it the peace of God.

The question of the therapeutic value of religion has long interested me. As you know, I came into the Church shortly after undergoing psychotherapy—a kind of halfway house, and I wanted to go the rest of the way. Psychotherapy promised a reconstruction of my personality, a dynamic reorientation. It can rearrange, but it cannot fulfill. So, at least unconsciously, I looked to religion to finish the job. After I first experienced God, I soon recognized that He Himself was all there was to be desired; that strength, comfort, security, peace of mind were all gifts which would be added unto me. They were merely by-products of a life in God. I would have got nowhere had I sought them first. It is somewhat like a man who wooed his beloved for herself alone and later is agreeably surprised to find that she can also cook and sew and has a little income of her own. If he loves truly, the added values will be of secondary importance or none at all. The primary concern is not what God is doing for us, but what we are doing for Him.

I cannot help being distressed whenever I see the love of God being subordinated to "happiness psychology," such as we hear from Norman Vincent Peale. A system which reduces religion to "techniques" for achieving a "calm philosophy of life" or a "scientific procedure for successful living" is, in my opinion, a travesty of Christianity. Even the power of prayer is classed as an "efficiency method." A man who was nervous, distressed, and spiritually bankrupt went to Dr. Peale for help. This is what happened:

> Of course it was necessary to teach this man a new pattern of thinking and acting. This was done in part by suggesting literature written by experts in the field of spiritual culture. For example, we gave him lessons in the skill of church going. We showed him how to make church worship a therapy. He was instructed in the scientific use of prayer and relaxation. And as a result of this practice eventually he became a healthy man.[12]

No doubt he did become a "healthy" man, but did he become a religious man, a lover of God and his fellows? The Christian, too, receives health of body and mind in his relationship to God and his dependence upon God, not dependence upon his own efforts in working out "techniques" for his own salvation. It may be good therapy, but is it good religion? What will happen when that man is faced with a new crisis—will his "efficiency methods" suffice? Religion is most assuredly not a science; the ways of God cannot be predicted; the will of God cannot be utilized to serve our own ends.

What about spiritual healing? Since our Church has done a great deal to promote the use of the Sacrament of Healing, this, too, has been a subject of great interest to me. I have not been able to reach any definite conclusions about it, but I do have some relevant impressions and opinions.

The practice of healing man's body and mind was an integral part of Christ's ministry and He made definite arrangements for that work to be continued, but during the centuries following, the Church neglected it so much that we wound up with something that was done only at man's last hour on earth—Extreme Unction, it was called.* There are, of course, many isolated examples of healing by faith which, like the miracles of Lourdes, have been carefully documented and attested to, but it was not until the last decade that any great interest was aroused in the Sacrament's healing aspect. Today many churches in this country and throughout the world have regular services of spiritual healing; the results are often thrilling.

I don't believe you can fairly dismiss the subject of spiritual healing without first examining the growing body of evidence. People sometimes seem to joke about clipping the wings of the Holy Dove, but it is just another instance in which we have presumed to limit God's power by confining it to small, "appropriate" areas. (However, I think the Church is wise in refusing to publicize its healing power; after all, it is but one aspect of our Lord's ministry.)

Many Churchmen, in various parts of the world, have done a great deal to uncover the Church's healing power, but I have been especially impressed with Emily Gardiner Neal's extensive study as set forth in her book, *A Reporter Finds God Through Spiritual Healing*.[13] She has approached everything with clear eyes and with the attitude of a thoroughgoing skep-

---

* Extreme Unction is not to be mistaken for the Sacrament of Unction. The former is a Romish rite administered at one's last, or extreme, hours; the latter is a sacrament administered during an illness. See Prayer Book, p. 320.—ED.

tic and unbeliever. I have an especially warm place in my heart for anyone who has "seen the light"!

One difficulty remains, and it may be explained on the basis of insufficient faith. There is a kind of "leftist" group in the Church which is so filled with enthusiasm that its people go so far as to say that God never wills pain and suffering, and that given enough faith and patience any cure can be effected. Certainly faith is of the essence; Christ insists again and again that "thy faith hath made thee whole."[14] The trouble is, though, that physical wholeness seems to be the end. Consequently I find myself on the "rightist" or more moderate side. Father John told me about visiting a hopelessly crippled parishioner who was so filled with gratitude and love of God, so actively engaged in helping others, that he, our priest, came away with the feeling that *he* had gained from the encounter. "I have never known anyone so whole," he said.

I am becoming more and more convinced that God often utilizes our infirmities as an implement of grace. I think a conundrum arises only when we become dogmatic about what is good and what is evil. God does not wish evil for us —that we know; but can we always know what constitutes our good? You know, of course, that I have an incurable disease which can only be arrested. In the first fit of despair I did a great deal of complaining, but my affliction soon became a leaven to my growth, and I was newly motivated to seek out God in areas where I had never needed Him before. Now I am truly thankful for what I once considered downright evil. It has forced me to rearrange myself, to replace one set of habits with another, to adopt new values in place of the ones I had outgrown, and to drive myself to explore the painful inroads of my own weakness. How could I not be grateful for such a challenge? I might have gone on for years without the slightest thought of trying to lead a fully Christian life. As long as we can "make out," as long as the rewards and losses seem to balance each other, the necessity to change is not apparent. Many are happily content with the answer which St. Paul was given: "My grace is sufficient for thee: for my strength is made perfect in weakness."[15] And it always is.

Of course, any idea of healing which denies the reality of evil and pain (as with Christian Scientists) is utterly un-Christian. How can we deny evil and pain and at the same time proclaim Christ's redeeming sacrifice? The Bible tells us clearly that it is by His stripes we are healed and through His suffering we are reconciled unto God. Faith-healing cults which discourage people who are seriously ill from seeking medical attention are, again, presuming to limit God. These days, no less than in Biblical days, the Spirit's healing grace comes to us through many channels.

This brings me back again to the necessity of relinquishing ourselves into God's care. You are no doubt weary of hearing me say it so often! If I could honestly come up with any other conclusion, I would. I find it hard to be original; every discovery of mine has turned out to be what believers in every generation have learned and passed on to others. It is indeed "the faith which was once delivered unto the saints."[16] And I don't think you will meet with much success in changing it to suit yourself.

You keep saying, "If Christianity were such and such, I would buy it!" Jesus said that it is a "strait . . . gate" and a "narrow . . . way"; perhaps that is why He added, "and few there be that find it."[17]

Your interest extends beyond taking Bob's courses in philosophy; it is personal, and it is becoming more urgent. Pascal recognized our serious predicament by emphasizing our forced option. Skepticism has value only when it leads to a decision; our very unwillingness to come to a decision is in itself a choice. So, while I admire you for your intellectual integrity, your eagerness to look on all sides of the question, I know you will not long be satisfied with a condition of indecision. A man without belief is in a state of suspended animation, since the direction of all his actions depends on that in which he has his faith. Faith has many objects besides God. Almost four years ago I decided that the objects of my faith were unworthy, and that my religious situation was actually a state of dishonesty, proceeding more from an unwillingness to be involved than from any rational reservations. Of course, I wouldn't have admitted this to anyone, but in my heart I knew it was true. This does not flatter our ego; but then, Christianity never does!

To end on a note of concord, let me say that I am in wholehearted agreement with you when you reject the nonchalant school of thought which declares that it doesn't make much difference what we believe so long as we believe something! Like you, I have sought, believing that I might find, the Truth. I am convinced that Truth is Almighty God as revealed through and in and by His Son. I cannot but hope that you will find the same.

XI

Letter to Priscilla

Santa Barbara, California
Monday, August 24, 1959

Dear Priscilla,

Since you are my next-door neighbor and have attended our church, seeking a spiritual home of your own, it was easy for me to confide in you my decision to become associated with one of our communities. I was amused at your remark, when I said I was going to spend a few days at a convent; you exclaimed, "Oh, *really!*" in the same tone of voice you might have used had I said that I was going to visit an opium den. It wasn't long ago that I myself knew little about the various Religious Orders in the Episcopal Church and, since you asked me to find out all I could about them and pass the information on, I thought I would write about it.

Two years ago I learned that we had such communities in our Church when I met the Mother Superior of the community of St. Saviour, in San Francisco. I was curious, as I am about everything pertaining to our Church, but the facts that I gleaned then seemed to have very little to do with me personally. Shortly afterwards I met Sisters Veronica, Mary Barbara, and Magdala of St. Mary's in Reno, a Roman community of the Dominican Order. I was delighted to find someone with whom I could share my love of God and learn more about the richer dedication of my life. I was growing alarmed

186

at the evidences of God's grace, fearful of becoming "odd," of being thought peculiar, and I hesitated at being more involved, too deeply committed. If Sunday churchgoing were enough for others, why not for me? Then my pride went to work and I began to imagine that God must find me especially lovable since He was lavishing so much upon me, and I began to feel "set apart"; but that state of affairs proved too uncomfortable and too much at variance with fact to last very long. The Sisters at St. Mary's, in Reno, helped me to put my relationship with God in focus by seeing it as nothing unusual. I was then able to relate all my religious experiences without hesitation, and they seemed to understand exactly what I was talking about.

Then it was that I felt the need to participate somehow in a religious community. This summer I met an associate of the Sisters of the Holy Nativity at our Church camp at Lake Tahoe and learned that it was possible for a lay person to be associated with one of our communities, to visit them and share in their common life, to make retreats, to join them in intercessory prayer, to follow a Rule of Life. I eagerly made inquiries, embarked upon a sea of correspondence, and eventually made arrangements to visit two or three of the closest Branch Houses on my way down to Southern California for my sister's wedding.

All of that gives you a little of the background of how it was I grew interested in our Religious Orders and their life.

August 25, 1959
Tuesday

I arrived here in Santa Barbara yesterday to visit St. Mary's Retreat House. This is a branch of the community of the

Sisters of the Holy Nativity of which I spoke and, after comparing their way of life and their Rule with those of other communities, I decided that this was my choice. I will, therefore, limit my descriptions to this particular community. It will not be a study of the religious life in general, but rather the impressions of an "ordinary pilgrim."

You have told me how dear to your heart Santa Barbara is, so I may revive some happy memories by describing St. Mary's. It is located on a hill with the mountains rising behind it, clothed in mist, surrounded by a terrace, gardens, and rustic walks, and permeated by the unforgettable odor of eucalyptus. The House itself is charming and spacious, and my room, named after St. Scholastica, overlooks a wooded scene with mountains in the background.

I was quite shy at first, and, of course, confused by all the different bells—some ours and some from the Mission nearby. A formidable timetable was presented to me, and I was left to get on with it. Camp Galilee had prepared me for a scheduled life and, believe me, without children and K. P., it is a life of leisure!

The bells are enchanting. One has a deep, somber voice that is answered by her sister, a serene treble, and the two are accompanied by a prankish peal that runs in and out like a laughing child. What a pleasure it is to kneel in the quiet chapel under the blinking eye of the sanctuary lamp, with the votive candles flickering a soft glow on the statue of the Madonna and Child. The exquisite wood carving on the altar, the tapestry behind, the gilded crucifix, the dark overhead beams—all add to the delight of just being here. Even the silence is bright and sunny, and of course there is a feeling of mystery and love. When we went to Grace Church Cathedral in San Francisco, my husband remarked that Christ would surely have been horrified at such opulence, no matter how inspiring. As I knelt in the nave of that splendid cathedral church, as in the modest little chapel at St. Mary's, I could not help but think that our own lives ought to bear the burden of poverty, but that the houses of God should be made beautiful and speak of His glory—after all, a church is God's house, and through stone and wood, silk and silver, color and light, we praise Him and are drawn closer to His presence.

I am sure that all the individual "helps" we resort to in our worship are justifiable when they bring us closer to God. For example, the graceful *prie-dieu* which Father Ted gave me, and which you have often admired, has been an enormous aid to me in "recollection"—helping me to focus my mind and my will upon God in prayer.

Here at Santa Barbara we are surrounded by such beauty on every side that I must write about it. The eucalyptus trees fascinate me. Their trunks are colored delicately, but quite surprisingly, with taupe, aqua, and pink. One of our visitors commented that if we were to see such trees on a stage we would think that the set designer was a bit touched. It seems to me that people, like everything else that only God can make, turn out just as unlikely. The saying that truth is stranger than fiction is nowhere more fitting than in the religious life—all my experiences have been simply unbelievable!

But back to our schedule. We arise early, and I mean early. The rising bell clangs at 6:30 and, for those visitors who can make it, the first Office, Prime, is read at 6:45. The Holy Communion is celebrated at 7:15. The service is a bit more "high church" than that to which I am accustomed. Curiously enough, the Creed is omitted on weekdays because, I am told, it has been said silently before. It seems to me that if anything should be said aloud it's the Creed. It should be said standing and out loud because it is, literally, what we "stand for." However, as in all our parishes, things differ here and there, but that is unimportant.

Next is breakfast, in silence. Silence is maintained from after Compline the night before until after breakfast. I don't know what there is about silence that, for me—and others, I hear—is so conducive to laughter. Riley Gibson, another visitor, and one with whom I have become well acquainted, and I are a disastrous combination. It all started after Compline last night, as we were munching our crackers in silence. (Graham crackers and milk are left for us as a bedtime snack.) We just happened to look at each other and immediately started laughing. During Vespers today we were at our worst. Vespers is my undoing anyway; it changes every day, and I can never find my place. Riley manages beautifully and somehow always knows just where we are. I tell her she must do it by radar! At any rate, she was amused at my frantic fumbling with the book, and I happened to catch the expression on her face; from then on neither of us dared open our mouths for fear that we would break into another spell of laughter. Really, I haven't giggled in church since I was thirteen! But they tell me this, too, is "par for the course." They also tell me that the habit of silence is rewarding, but I haven't got that far yet. Right now it all seems so awkward.

At 9:15 we have Terce and Sext combined, and then follows a free period until noon. The Sisters have so many worth-while books in their library that I am leaving with a whole page full of titles. Most of them, I am told, can be borrowed by anyone from the convent's library in Fond du Lac, Wisconsin, for only the cost of postage. O happy day! Now I can read to my heart's content. Just think—all this was within my reach, and I didn't know about it until now!

At noon the Angelus bell is rung, and the Office of None is read. Then lunch and a free afternoon. At six is Vespers, followed by dinner, another free period, Compline, and then bed. The nuns read Lauds later so they won't have to get up in the middle of the night, but I never stayed for that.

Roughly, that is the schedule. It all sounds rather full and possibly uninviting, but it isn't really. The Offices are quite brief; they last only about fifteen or twenty minutes. We, as visitors, are not required to attend all the Offices. While the day is full, there is plenty of time to be by oneself, to talk with the other guests or, for that matter, to go off shopping or sightseeing. Expenses are not high; at the conclusion of a stay a guest leaves an offering of whatever he can afford and wants to leave.

It was one whole day before I had a chance to speak to any of the Sisters. They are all very busy, especially now because two of their members were transferred to another House, and since they have not been immediately replaced, the Sisters are short-handed. How do so few of them manage to run Retreat House, prepare and serve meals, attend seven Offices, to say nothing of the Eucharist, make hospital calls, say their intercessions, write their letters, and do heaven knows how many other things? It is even more amazing that they manage to accomplish so much and at the same time appear to be involved in something eternal.

At first it was all rather unnerving to me, coming as I did from a wedding and shortly before that a visit to my home in Alhambra—my first visit since my mother's death. The phrase "the slow, awful patience of God" comes to mind. Here I was, being so conscious of time going by, filled with questions, on tiptoe with eagerness, only to be met with an undeviating cycle of chapel, meals, silence, and more chapel.

I had planned to waylay one Sister after Compline last night only to find that the "Great Silence" had descended. This afternoon I tried to catch another but was outmaneuvered by her stride. She seemed to move so unhurriedly and quietly that I figured I could catch up with her rather easily, but she was out of sight before I reached the door of the chapel. I doubt now if I could have made it on a dead run!

But today I did manage to talk with the Sister Superior simply by being doorkeeper for her so that she could take a nap! My reward was our conversation. I had been alarmed by her statement which I had overheard her make to another aspirant, "We like to know people about a year before we consider them for lay associates." A year! Apparently I was able to convince her that my decision was not capricious or sudden, for although she did not commit herself one way or another, she did say that she would write to the Mother Superior about me this fall.

I see now that all the time I was being observed. Remembering my behavior of the last twenty-four hours, I can't imagine on what grounds I could be recommended. So, *mea culpa*: I had lurched into the refectory (those polished floors!) almost late, I had caused one of the Sisters to break the silence by asking me to pass food which I should have thought to pass anyway, I had kept my lights on after "lights out," I had smoked in my room before I realized smoking was forbidden, I had gone into the chapel without my "chapel cap," I had clattered down the stairs, I had "visited" with one of the guests in her room (that was also forbidden), during three of the Offices I had read altogether the wrong responses. Besides that, I am always dropping things. By bedtime last night I had almost decided there was nothing here for me.

Moving among people who are so tidy, so regulated, so

composed, so holy, can be a forbidding and disillusioning experience. Perhaps that's the idea—to take any Sarah Bernhardt out of one's performance. Anyway, today I have felt much more at home. I am reminded of how I felt when I began going to church, how I never could find my place in the Prayer Book, and how (there's the bell for Vespers—have to run—) foreign everything seemed to me. Now I feel quite comfortable at any service; perhaps a day will come when I can feel equally at ease reading the Divine Offices with a group of nuns and walking across the world's slickest floor.

Wednesday, August 26, 1959

Things are settling down now. I feel much more at home and there is more conversation between the guests and the Sisters, and I have been doing some visiting with the other guests. Our questions and problems are different, of course, yet there is a common core of interests. One visitor is asking almost the same questions that were troubling me a year ago. Another is years ahead of us all and is quite a storehouse of information.

Visitors come from many places and for many reasons. One young woman has been in a sanitarium for a nervous breakdown and her week's visit here was designed to bridge her dependent life in the sanitarium and the responsible life at home. Another woman, older and much more mature, is here because she has hit a "dry spell" in her spiritual life and wishes to be refreshed. Another is here on a vacation from an overly demanding job. Most of the guests will be going into retreat, which begins Friday. One woman wants to see whether or not she should become a nun. Another thought she wanted to become a lay associate but has decided that after all she doesn't. What she really wants is a Rule of Life, not association with the community. I, on the other hand, am relieved to find that a Rule of Life is incidental to association and corporate worship—which is what I am really after. I am feeling more and more that this is what I need and want, and, God willing, it may be mine.

As for my feelings of unworthiness, I usually find them to be the backside of pride. So I tell myself, of course you can't be expected to be polished and perfected in this kind of life because this is your first go at it, so stop all this nonsense about not being up to everything and push on as best you can. And for heaven's sake, I tell myself, stop being so egotistical as to imagine that everybody here—especially the Sisters—is watching you out of the corner of her eye. That's one nice thing about growing in faith, you aren't bogged down with nearly so much; for example, it grows harder to deceive yourself.

It's a pity I have to leave tomorrow, just when I am beginning to learn the routine and feel so much at ease in these pleasant surroundings. I'm afraid I've been a little too interested and eager to take full advantage of the opportunities for rest, meditation, and prayer. I've been far too busy learning, too busy satisfying my curiosity. Oh well, next time I'll have all that behind me and can really "settle down." If I am ever to be received as an associate of this community I'd like to precede my reception with a retreat. So many "firsts"—and what an adventure the religious life is!

But what about convent life and what's it like? I can hear you ask that, but I don't think I can answer you very well, because it's not so much a kind of living as it is a *quality* of living. My impression of the nuns came not especially from what they say but more what they do, and how they do it. Essentially, they serve God and others, but everything they do is done with pleasure, with reverence, with gentleness—or so it seems to me. I seldom find them actually doing anything, and so there is some mystery about what is done. Clean sheets are waiting where they can be found, the table is always set, the books are placed on the chapel table with markers to indicate the proper places. You have only to ask a passing question on, say, some aspect of the Church's doctrine, and a book will appear to provide the answer. It reminds me of the story of the shoemaker and the elves!

But it's not a "natural life," you protest. No, it isn't; it's a "supernatural life"—an answer Rosemary Howard-Bennett gives in her book, *I Choose the Cloister*.[1] My casual and brief visits to St. Mary's in Reno were confined to the parlor and the garden, with an occasional visit to the chapel during one of the Offices—always said in Latin and therefore something I could not understand. I had no intimate glimpse of the lives of the professed. I don't know if you have such prejudice, but many people feel that nuns are dreary and stern, that they are escapists or dismally pious, often "disappointed in love." Nothing could be further from the truth. Collectively, they are an uncommonly happy lot; individually, their differences are more or less what we would expect to find in any group of people. One will have a good sense of humor, another will be tender and winning, and another all efficiency and common sense. I can't see that the religious life has standardized them at all.

The monastic life is no more than obedience to Christ's admonition to sell your possessions, give the money to the poor, and build up a treasure in heaven. How, then, can the religious life be considered selfish or eccentric? It is simply living the Christian life fully.

A *Testament of Turning*

I cannot but wish that all parish priests would inform their people about the life and work of our monks and nuns, and say at least something about the opportunities such Orders provide for all Church people. An occasional word from the pulpit or a pamphlet in the tract rack would help greatly. Here again, as with sacramental confession, I did not know we had monks and nuns in our Church until two years ago; and from all that I've gathered, my experience is not uncommon. At least we ought to know about them, and their associates, and what they are doing and why. A Sister of another community told me that she had a great deal of difficulty coming by any information about Religious Orders and, when she did get it, it was scant and apparently grudgingly provided. I suspect that there are many young people, here and there in various parishes throughout the United States, who have a very real vocation to the religious life, but are never given an opportunity to discover it. In my own case, I'd been searching a long time without knowing what I was looking for. People who wish a fuller religious life can best acquire what they are seeking by the discipline found in a Rule of Life, and each Order has one for dedicated lay people. After all, one cannot be fully obedient unless one has something to be obedient to, and if one is left to his own devices his prayer life cannot be effective without some kind of orderliness. A sanctified life cannot be attained without direction.

Thursday, August 27, 1959

This afternoon I will return home, to take up my life "in the world"—sharpened, quickened, and refreshed. How did I come by so much? Was it in conversation with the Sisters, in finding spiritual direction, in the fellowship of other visitors, in being hidden in Christ, away from the distractions and pressures of daily life, in the recitation of the Divine Office, in opportunities for rest and prayer, in the beauty of these surroundings? I think all of these have contributed to my refreshment. But more than anything else, just dwelling closer to God, in an atmosphere of holy quiet and meditation, best fits us for a vigorous renewal of our work, of our personal relationships, and our growth in Him who said that we must be in, but not of, this world.

I do hope the Sisters will have me as an associate of their Order.

October 2, 1959

You said you wanted to know how I felt after I had had time to "marinate," as you put it, my visit to the Sisters. Well, since I have been confined to bed ever since I returned home with an ugly virus, believe me, it has had plenty of time to marinate! In fact, I have been unable to do anything but think (and that not very clearly) in the last few weeks.

Of course, I still want very much to become an associate of a community, but like so many other things, nothing has happened—yet. At St. Mary's I learned how to live in God's time, but my recent illness has put a stop to everything. There were moments when I did not know what was going to be required of me—perhaps even my life! At such times we see the unimportance of so many of our activities, our possessions, and even our aspirations. What we hold dear when our lives are endangered is singled down to our relationship with people and with God. It is a time of stocktaking, of sincere recollection, a period of great patience, of being calm when things are stormy. For example, my neglect of the household led to innumerable domestic problems; since I was unable to supervise them, the children grew fretful and got into all sorts of mischief. I had to make up my mind to make no plans whatever for the future, to revoke our social commitments, and to accept the probability that what had now become my book would fail to be finished on time. Little by little I was stripped of everything I had counted on, hoped for, and had taken for granted.

Most discouraging of all was the realization that I was deprived of any real contact with God. For a while I was too ill to say my customary prayers, and could only repeat over and over again God's Name. But, curiously, as I became physically weaker I became spiritually stronger. My faith waxed as my energy waned. In the pit of pain and suffering we come to know God in an entirely different way—no, perhaps it's the same way, but when we are stripped of almost all our senses, all our ideas, and our customary conveniences, we learn more about the soul—about our real selves. When our body seems to come apart, when our mind is wearied and all our senses leave us—when we seem to have nothing left, we can know God all the better. The security we find in the midst of sickness is far greater than what we find "whilst [we] are in health." Truly, there is nothing God can give to us or take from us that is not a blessing—ultimately.

Now that I am well again, shall I forget the lessons I learned? Shall I become again frantically busy and fret over projects and events and things? Shall I try to accomplish too much all at once? Shall I grow dismayed at my failures and be frustrated by small disappointments? Shall I return to despair when I fall out of touch with God? Yes, I'm afraid so. But less, always less so. At each point in our growth in

God we retain the heart of our lessons, and that is what germinates the whole field. When we seem to be dormant, spiritually or physically, we have only to remember that even the best soil has to lie fallow once in a while.

To answer your question, yes—I received yesterday the manual of the Sisters of the Holy Nativity and my probation period will start after Christmas.

XII

Letter to Father Ted

All Saints' Day, 1959

Dear Father Ted:

The first of these letters was written to the priest who planted that first seed in my mind. So it is only appropriate that the last letter should be written to you, my confessor, and the one who is generously helping to bring in the harvest of that random planting.

Lately I have been reading over these letters, organizing them, and correcting them with the thought that they may qualify for publication. The revising and cropping has given me a pretty good view of the whole incredible experience. I am both startled and pleased. I am beginning to see why people don't, as a rule, do this sort of thing—it's much too embarrassing. Some parts of it are hard for me to believe, and some parts I'd just as soon deny. But above all is the temptation to delete the sections that speak of brashness and confusion.

I find myself wishing that I could have another six months, another year; but really, what would that add? Another period of growth, of course, but I am beginning to have the uneasy feeling that I would not, at the conclusion of another year, be able to come up with anything greatly different from what went before. I am sure, however, that I would have better sense than to put it all down on paper! There is a tendency to become less subjective as we proceed. Then, too, the past is always less important than the present or the future.

I have recounted the experience of only one person. If a geologist were to send down an auger to take a core, a sample of a particular stratum in a particular section of the earth, he would come up with a specimen of layer upon layer, all indicating growth in a recurring pattern. There is really no satisfactory place to stop in an account of the religious life for the very good reason that, once the force which brings a person into close relation to God has started, there is no stopping place. Christ alone can say when "it is finished."

We never know when anything is really ended; we know only that we view things differently and that they seem to change. In the beginning I was only a spectator, and I could look at my own experience with some objectivity; now I am deeply involved, and my perspective has changed. It is harder now to discuss my experiences; there is a certain shyness that springs up, a hesitancy, a caution. Nevertheless, I am going to try to be a spectator again, and look at the last four years as if they had happened to someone else.

It would be impossible to mention, or even find, all the changes. If they aren't already apparent to the reader, I have failed as a writer. In rereading the letters I find that one change has not been dealt with adequately: that is, as my religion takes on more meaning, I take myself less seriously, and that inevitably affects my response to God. I used to suppose that God had to be approached with some solemnity, but now I see that the utmost simplicity will do as well. I once looked upon the glad, presumptuous abandon of St. Teresa of Lisieux, for example, as rather lacking in the proper appreciation of God's glory. Another paradox: we can never grow large enough to accommodate God, for the more we grow the smaller we become. The child of God who abandons himself into his Father's keeping with the most simplicity is likely to see most deeply into the mysteries of God.

In becoming less solemn in my religious habits and thinking, I have acquired a joy—almost a prankish joy—that I had not known since my childhood. It is a merriment born of the memory of myself evoked by these letters. As I review these letters and glimpse a picture of myself I am astonished to find the ham actor, strutting and posturing; the humbled supplicant, bending the knee and bowing the head; the sainted soul, elated and exalted—I laughed until the tears came! My fantasies had clothed me in so many costumes that I was like the child in *The Emperor's New Clothes;* I could see at last the pretense that covered my nakedness.

Now laughter punctuates my prayers. Now I can bring anything to God, even my own foolish self. I learned, furthermore, that I can bring my anger. If we are to have a truly personal relationship with God, we cannot exclude our emotions—any of them. It would be absurd to pretend that we are not occasionally angry with God. (Actually we are angry with ourselves, and that is the anger I am talking about.) His will cannot at all times be uniformly pleasing to us. We will be irritable, resentful, rebellious, and even defiant. What are we to do with such emotions? Hide them from Him who is the Designer of our nature, the Searcher of our hearts? We can try to repress such feelings, but when we do we invite trouble. God calls to us, as He did to Adam, and asks why we hide. I learned first that I could bring my doubt. Then, cautiously, fearfully, I brought my hostility. As no bolts of lightning struck me down, I continued to do so. I have never had the slightest indication that it was not a fit and proper thing to do. Indifference, not anger, weakens relationships. It is evasion that breeds guilt and separation. When we learn how to deal with God honestly, many things are simplified.

For example, I think we are constantly hampered by erroneous ideas of what a religious life ought to be. You once likened spurious forms of the religious life to a tent that was not securely anchored, just so much "flapping canvas." An acquaintance of Bob's and mine has told us, apparently quite seriously, that he doesn't pray because he doesn't want to "bother God." I told him the truth was that he doesn't want to be bothered with God! I used to think that for anyone to ask God for a great deal of help, or for anyone to aspire to sainthood, was audacious and presumptuous; now I see that my attitude, which I thought was one of humility, was merely laziness. I'm glad you agree with me in taking issue with those who think of mysticism as an emotive and celestial affair—something unrealistic. Actually, mysticism is simply enjoying the love of God, believing that we can find the Ineffable and know the Unknowable. For those who see God as the Source of reality, it seems to me that mysticism is the only sensible answer. In any event it is the only way I have of piercing through that "cloud of unknowing" to find Him.

I'm not having nearly so much trouble with the mysteries of Christianity as I expected. All the theological dither about such matters leaves me quite puzzled, which indicates either a lack of comprehension and sophistication or that I have somehow stumbled upon a simpler access to Truth.

Why should the Incarnation be so surprising? Why, if we start with the divinity of God, should it amaze us that He could for His own purposes also assume humanity—which He Himself created?

Why should the Resurrection be such a puzzle? Why, when with the greatest confidence in the world, we perennially plant an apparently dead seed in the ground and without question expect it to rise and flower into a new life?

Why should we stumble at the idea of receiving our Lord in the creaturely elements of bread and wine? Why, when we clearly see that a gift from a beloved person can be far more than a bit of lace and cloth—that it also contains a formidable part of the giver and his love? Where is the dancer after the music dies away? Where the author after the pages of his book are closed? Is the dancer not in the dance and the writer in his ideas, both living simultaneously a life apart from the manifestations of themselves?

Why do we balk at the doctrine of the Trinity? Why, when we ourselves harbor within us different personalities? I am, at one and the same time, both a poet and an academician: to me a metaphor is as high a form of truth as a geometric theorem. We do not have to be a Dr. Jekyll-Mr. Hyde to be aware of the various personality struggles within ourselves. Not only do we have different personalities, but we have separate selves: we have a mind, a body, and a soul—each serves a different function and yet each is commingled with the others. And how do we see, determine, prove that they exist? By our own experience of them, by the testimony of others, by common consent. Are our souls, our persons, that ineffable part of ourselves, the less real because they cannot be examined in a laboratory?

It seems to me that God has given us the best possible means by which we can apprehend these mysteries—ourselves. We cannot understand them, much less understand ourselves, but we can know ourselves as we can know God, and in that knowing—find. I think it is a knowledge that actually has very little to do with reason: we apprehend ourselves much in the same way that we apprehend God, through that commonly called "sixth sense" which is none other than our spirit. Does that mean that our senses are therefore not a part of our spiritual apparatus? The case of Helen Keller shows how impossible it is to eliminate the causative and vital force behind our senses. A sixth sense—fully free, unbound and without bodily restraint—might very well perform the function of the other five.

The mysteries of God—His miracles—are they confined to God alone? Don't they spill over and permeate every aspect of His creation, especially in ourselves and in our daily human relationships? We take them for granted simply because they are commonplace. We will never see the mysteries of God, behold His miracles, so long as we insist that God, who made us, is less than ourselves. If even we bear traces of these divine mysteries, how much less surprised shall we be to find that Almighty God has and does exactly what He claims, and that—with even a small amount of willing perceptiveness— His mysteries can be revealed to us in all their fullness.

Later

Having just come from confession, I've been thinking about holiness. I know several people who have it; you are one of them. And I want to have it, too. (I'm sorry, but absolution makes me audacious!) I am coming to see that holiness is something one acquires from God over a long period of time. One can be sanctified in a moment, but one cannot become holy in a moment. Holiness is like a rock that the sea washes over. It stays there, obdurate, faithful, day after day, year after year. The tide comes up and covers it. The spume obscures it, seems to obliterate it altogether, but when the surf has burst and the tide recedes we see that it still remains securely anchored. I am like the sand. I try to make a stand against the sea of my own weakness, but you see how foolish that is!

Meredith asked me a question the other day that I couldn't answer. She said, "After you go to confession aren't you forgiven?" "Yes, certainly." "But," she continued, "aren't you really all clean then?" "Yes," I replied, more wary now. "Then, if you made your confession just before you died, why wouldn't everyone go straight to heaven?"

I'm sorry to say I dodged that one and meant to ask you later. The logic of it seemed right, but something was amiss somewhere. Now I know. Now I could say something like this to her: You know how ridiculous Mark looks when he puts on Daddy's shoes? Well, that's the way it is. Mark isn't ready to be a man yet. This has nothing to do with how good he is—he may be better in the sight of God than Daddy. I may be better in the sight of God than a lot of people—the moment I leave the confessional. In fact, that's the only time I ever am. But that doesn't make me ready for heaven. I have a very small soul and it has to grow, enormously, before I can stand in the presence of God.

This is probably not very good theology, but it's what I'd say to Meredith. Right at this moment I am, through the Sacrament of Penance, sanctified. It is a delight and a joy to know that the Holy Spirit dwells again in me, that the lines of communication are open. I am free, and a geyser of hope shoots up in me. Death no longer seems real. I live, briefly, in life eternal. This will not last for longer than a few hours, a few days at the most. I don't mean that I will drop like a stone into limbo. Separation from God takes a while. But, sooner or later, I'll get there. I shall break my vows again. I shall reject God, desert Him, deny Him—as I am, going from one transient period of sanctification to another. Therefore I must change: I must become holy.

I don't think it's something I can pray for, because as I understand it, it isn't given to us in a lump sum, as a single gift. It's many, many smaller gifts which we come by in the hardest possible way—the way Evelyn Underhill came by them—faithful, dogged service, daily emptying of self, the only kind of action we can ever take to facilitate our growth. Joy in the love of God is a precious thing, and I would be the last to disparage it. But I can see now that it will never give me the nourishment I need to make the stand it seems God intends me to take. The kind of security that rocks enjoy is not enhanced by eruptions.

Oh, I know my spiritual candle power is not dependent upon brilliant displays. I've learned to trim my wick very closely and dwell in near darkness for months on end. But it's always that one last day without the Light which I cannot bear; yet I must learn how to bear it, because it is always that one last day of darkness which God accepts and turns into radiance. Then each of those dim days added together will lead to holiness. And in the process I shall learn a kind of Braille so that, though sightless, I may still be able to "practise the presence of God."

God has taught me something today through you. I've started to learn something about holiness. I don't think it's anything I'll ever be able to enjoy; in fact, once I acquire it, I'll probably never know I've got it. I'll never be able to write books about it! But it is what I need to have, maybe not for my salvation, but for my survival—and, frankly, I'm more concerned with the latter right now. The rest will follow in God's own good time.

I am sorry it has taken me so long. As with one's beloved,

we wonder how we ever existed before he came into our lives; as with our children, we wonder how we ever managed without them (yes, even when we wonder how we can ever manage *with* them); so it is with God—we wonder how we ever lived even for a moment without Him, without knowing Him, without His presence.

The convert occasionally agonizes over his former emptiness, his selfishness, his long-standing indifference. When I was a skeptic it was incredible to me that anyone took the existence of God for granted. Now that I am a believer, I find it impossible to take Him for granted. I, who almost failed to find Him, can never quite lose the fear of losing Him. I know you wish I would relax a little here!

But there is one reason why I could not have made my search earlier. I had first to gain a certain maturity and a certain freedom. Only free people can give themselves. Then, too, growth is from the roots up. We cannot change ourselves by hacking away at the branches. We all attempt the futility of trying to change the core of ourselves by making superficial adjustments in our lives. We think that a change of job, a change of environment will do the trick. Some of us try to alter the climate of our souls by getting a divorce, having a baby, taking a trip, or embracing a new creed or a new set of values, only to discover that we have changed nothing vital in ourselves. For the health of our whole being, we must be firmly planted in God; all essential change takes place here— at the source of our life, in our roots.

I will admit that the religious quest need not be burdened with quite so many difficulties as I have encountered. I have tilted at a few windmills (my husband insists that I complicate all my experiences), but I do not think that for anyone who encounters God it can ever be an easy, casual, or insensate meeting; sooner or later it means confusion, loving, yearning, suffering, and sacrifice. That is the risk we take when we are invaded by His relentless love. It is a perilous adventure—or so it seems to me.

Some ask, "Is it worth it?" What a question! As I've said repeatedly, the love of God—even more, God's love for us— is worth all we have, and are, or ever hope to be.

Someone asked me a curious thing the other day. If none of this were true, he wanted to know, would I still be glad at my life's end that I had believed in God? Of course—look at all I've gained already! But my belief is involved in, and supported by, its own reality, so it is impossible, at this stage anyway, to make any analysis. Well then, he persisted, let us suppose that there is a God but that there is no life to come —that death settles all accounts, and that your evaluation must be made upon the basis of your earthly existence—would it then be worth it? Of course it would. My present joy and the fullness of it does not depend upon any future "rewards" or revelations. For the simple reason that I already exist in the "age to come," life now cannot be considered apart from life eternal. We who have had a glimpse of it know already too much about eternity to doubt it! When we put on the "new man" we have already begun the new life.

What I have come to believe is not a private or personal or individual matter: it is all contained in the Apostles' and the Nicene Creeds; it is the faith shared by the family of God —His Church. Someone is bound to exclaim, "That's what I thought, she's been wheedled into it!" I shall reply that these letters reveal only a small part of my former doubts, only a little of the research and the inquiries I made into the Christian faith, and only a little of the resistance I made to the whole business. I doubt if one could find a more stubborn, a more recalcitrant skeptic than I was at the start of my search.

It is right to be so. It is important—utterly necessary to have a sound foundation for one's belief—and that cannot be done by blind acceptance of what seems wrong and unreasonable. The Apostle Paul advises us: "Prove all things; hold fast that which is good."[1]

Christianity, at any stage, is a religion of personal experience; we have to learn piecemeal and for ourselves, through all avenues of investigation and above all on our own. Even those who have some faith to begin with should not hesitate to broaden it and bring it to maturity. We have to learn to lean on our faith, to test it in the fires of everyday life, to subject it to all kinds of pressures. If it doesn't bear up, it's not worth having.

An intelligent faith in Truth will always win out on its own merits. If it was planted in us as children, by our parents or by the Church, chances are that it will not, as it stands, be too sturdy when we reach adulthood; it needs the development that comes only by responding to all the challenges of the modern world. An apron-string faith will never do. I'm sure I will go on asking questions all my life; when new evidence arises to cast doubts on present convictions, they will have to be re-examined. And they should be. Dogmatism can be stultifying. We can never outgrow God. True freedom lies in comforming ourselves to the purposes for which we were made. I think we ought always to re-examine those purposes as we grow.

We cannot profitably undertake anything without God's help. As the Collect for the Nineteenth Sunday after Trinity asks: "O God, forasmuch as without thee we are not able to please thee; Mercifully grant that thy Holy Spirit may in all things direct and rule our hearts. . . . "

How do I feel now? Grateful—first to God who in His infinite mercy drew me to Himself, and then outward to all the people who helped me to search—and find; and grateful to all those who put up first with my temerity, then with my arrogance, and always with my questions. In recent months I have been especially grateful to you for bringing me back again and again to the simple, whole, unvarnished truth. You know well how I love to embellish and dramatize! You know well my tendency to be scrupulous: a trait that can lead, in the hands of a wise confessor, to a sensitive and steady conscience —and when left alone can strain at gnats but swallow camels. Common sense can also go pretty fast astray, but it can be relied on more than I had supposed!

What of the future? I shall kneel again in St. Stephen's (or in Trinity Church, or wherever it may be) and struggle with some particular problem . . . I shall be lonely and wish that my husband were beside me . . . I shall sing again in my low and cracked voice . . . I shall come to you for God's absolution and hope that you will not remember some of my shameful and whispered words . . . I shall come away clean and unfettered . . . I shall grow bored sometimes—during a sermon, a long prayer, or some particularly tedious Old Testament lesson . . . my mind will wander, but suddenly my heart will leap within me like a fish rising to the lure, and a wild, untamed joy will inundate me; I shall have a brief insight into what we are doing, and in that fleeting moment I will see that I am part of a whole Body, caught in history . . . I shall carry something of that glory back to my home . . . I shall look into the clear, inquiring eyes of my children and thank God for them . . . I shall remember people in my prayers . . . I shall become remote, imprisoned within myself . . . People will start to get on my nerves . . . I shall tire of the effort . . . I shall defy God again, and suffer again in the hell of separation . . . In tears I shall cry out, O Lord, have mercy, O Christ, have mercy! . . . I shall be restored . . . In my thanksgiving I shall try to prove myself worthy of the restoration . . . I shall become busy, and proud . . . I shall mastermind all my projects . . . I shall find peace nowhere . . . I shall come to laugh at myself, and again I shall be brought back into the circle of God's love . . . I shall grow distracted and be concerned with my own affairs, I shall lose contact with God . . . I shall become alarmed and anxious . . . I shall be in doubt and despair . . . I shall have faith in His presence, in His loving-kindness . . . In the fullness of God's time it will be rewarded . . . And I shall rejoice.

This is my pattern. I wish it were otherwise. I wish I could say that the time for doubt, for defiance, for despair, and for separation were over. For ten days after my mother's death I lived in such continuous prayer and in such close contact with God that I learned a great deal, I think, about the Kingdom of Heaven. It is during such periods that we wonder how we can ever live otherwise. It isn't only that we are stupid and ungrateful and defiant (if this were all, we should be unhappy creatures indeed!), but God in His very goodness can make a blessing out of our own evil. If we were left to our own devices we should have nothing but hell. But when God teaches us, we learn, even before we turn, that He is there to meet us; He will come running from afar off and greet us with compassion.

I came, I saw, I was conquered—by that Love. My name was Legion; I was in darkness and doubt and was given a name, and a purpose, and a self. I was at the meridian of my life; I cast no shadow, and was given substance. I stood alone and apart, and was given a Family. I was guilty, and was freely pardoned. I stood in peril, and was delivered. I was burdened with the ghosts of old sorrows, and was given joy to have and to hold.

Until we find God, it is night. But dawn comes up in every face, and as soon as the eyes have sight.

Acknowledgments

Acknowledgments

The Scripture quotations marked "R.S.V." are from the Revised Standard Version of *The Holy Bible*, copyrighted 1946, 1952, and 1957 by the Division of Christian Education, National Council of the Churches of Christ in the United States of America.

Letter I

1. Ezekiel 37:9.
2. St. Matthew 16:16.

Letter II

1. J. B. Phillips, *Your God Is Too Small*, The Epworth Press, London, 1952, and The Macmillan Company, New York, 1953, in chapter headings. Used with permission of The Epworth Press and The Macmillan Co.
2. C. S. Lewis, *Surprised by Joy*, Harcourt, Brace and Co., New York, 1955.
3. Gordon W. Allport, *The Roots of Religion*, Forward Movement Publications, Cincinnati, Ohio, p. 11.
4. "Meditation For a Young Boy Confirmed" by Alan Paton from October 13, 1954 issue. Copyright 1954 Christian Century Foundation. Reprinted by permission from *The Christian Century*.

Letter IV

1. "But as usually happens, the man who has tried a bad doctor is afraid to trust even a good one: so it was with the state of my soul, which could not be healed save by believing, and refused to be healed that way for fear of believing falsehood."—From *The Confessions of St. Augustine*, in the translation of F. J. Sheed, Copyright 1943 Sheed & Ward, New York, N. Y., p. 110.
2. Blaise Pascal, *Pensées*, E. P. Dutton and Co., Inc., New York, 1958, p. 17.

Letter V

1. Monica Baldwin, *I Leap Over the Wall*, Rinehart & Co., Inc., New York, 1950.
2. *Ibid.*
3. Genesis 32:26.
4. Lord Elton, *St. George or the Dragon*, William Collins Sons and Co., New York and Toronto, 1942.
5. Anne Morrow Lindbergh, *Gift from the Sea*, Pantheon Books, Inc., New York, 1955.
6. Baldwin, *op. cit.*
7. Hebrews 5:12-14.

Letter VI

1. From *The Complete Works of St. Teresa*, Translated and edited by E. Allison Peers from the critical edition of P. Silverio de Santa Teresa, C.D., Published in three volumes by Sheed & Ward, Inc., New York, 1946. Vol. I, p. 60.
2. *The Life of St. Teresa of Jesus*, Translated by David Lewis, published by Thomas Baker, London, 1916, and The Newman Press, Westminster, Maryland, 1943. Introduction by the Rev. Benedict Zimmerman, O.C.D.
3. St. Luke 5:32.
4. Peers, *op. cit.*, p. 75.
5. *Ibid.*, p. 47.
6. *Ibid.*, p. 77.
7. "When a soul finds itself exhausted and realizes clearly that it has no goodness of its own, when it feels ashamed in the presence of so great a King and sees how little it is paying of all that it owes Him, what need is there for it to waste its time on learning to know itself?"—*Ibid.*, p. 80.
8. "It is a very great thing always to bear this in mind, especially at first; later, we realize it so clearly that we need to forget it. . . . "—*Ibid.*, p. 93.
9. *Ibid.*, p. 74.
10. *Ibid.*, p. 73.
11. From *The Confessions of St. Augustine*, in the translation of F. J. Sheed, Copyright 1943 Sheed & Ward, New York, N. Y., p. 89.
12. *Ibid.*, p. 87.
13. *Ibid.*, p. 84.

14. ". . . I began to hold slackly and carelessly even the ideas with which I had decided to rest content while I could find nothing better."—*Ibid.*, p. 96.
15. *Ibid.*, p. 110.
16. *Ibid.*
17. *Ibid.*, p. 112.
18. *Ibid.*, p. 121.
19. *Ibid.*, p. 167.
20. *Ibid.*, p. 168.
21. *Ibid.*, p. 170.
22. *Ibid.*, p. 171.
23. *Ibid.*, p. 172.
24. *Ibid.*, p. 176.
25. *Ibid.*, p. 185
26. *Ibid.*, p. 189.
27. *Ibid.*, p. 215.
28. *Ibid.*
29. *Ibid.*, p. 219.
30. *Ibid.*, p. 233.
31. "See in what a state I am! Weep with me and weep for me, all you who feel within yourselves that goodness from which good actions come. Those of you who have no such feelings will not be moved by what I am saying. But do Thou, O Lord my God, hear me and look upon me and see me and pity me and heal me, Thou in whose eyes I have become a question to myself: and that is my infirmity."—*Ibid.*, p. 244.
32. "For it works its way into me with such power that if it is suddenly withdrawn, I desire it with great longing and if it is absent too long, it saddens my mind."—*Ibid.*

Letter VII

1. St. John 11:40.
2. St. Matthew 11:30.
3. Genesis 3:5, R.S.V.
4. Dorothy L. Sayers, *The Man Born to Be King*, Harper & Brothers, New York, 1949.
5. Genesis 3:5, R.S.V.
6. Harry Blamires, *The Will and the Way*, The Macmillan Company, New York, 1957, p. xi. © 1957 by Harry Blamires, and used with permission of The Macmillan Co.

7. St. John 6:68.
8. Josef Pieper, *Fortitude and Temperance*, Pantheon Books, Inc., New York, 1954.

Letter VIII

1. Psalms 46:1, 18:4, 66:9, 77:19, 91:5, 108:1, Book of Common Prayer.
2. I Corinthians 15:50.
3. I Corinthians 15:52.

Letter IX

1. *St. Bernard on the Love of God*, A. R. Mowbray & Co. Ltd., London, 1950, p. 13.
2. C. S. Lewis, *The Problem of Pain*, The Macmillan Company, New York, 1943, pp. 20-22. Used by permission of The Macmillan Co.
3. Isaiah 53:3.
4. Julian of Norwich.
5. "Job & J.B.," in *Time*, December 22, 1958, Section on "Religion."
6. Job 36:15, R.S.V.
7. Hebrews 10:31.
8. Dorothy L. Sayers, *The Mind of the Maker*, Harcourt, Brace and Co., New York, 1941. © 1941 Dorothy L. Sayers. Reprinted by permission A. Watkins, Inc.
9. Friedrich von Hügel, *Essays and Addresses*, First Series, "What Do We Mean by Heaven and Hell?" as quoted in C. S. Lewis, *The Problem of Pain*, p. 111, fn. 2.
10. Lord Acton, as quoted in a letter to Bishop Mandell Creighton, in Lord Acton's *Letters*, 1887.
11. St. Francis of Assisi.
12. Nicolas Berdyaev, *The Destiny of Man*, Geoffrey Bles, London, 1937.

Letter X

1. Paul Tillich, *The Protestant Era*, University of Chicago Press, Chicago, 1948, p. xi. Copyright 1948 by the University of Chicago.
2. From *The Confessions of St. Augustine*, in the translation of F. J. Sheed, Copyright 1943 Sheed & Ward, New York, N. Y., p. 3.

Acknowledgments

3. William Temple, *Nature, Man and God*, Macmillan & Co. Ltd., London, 1934, p. 54. Used by permission of Mrs. William Temple, Macmillan & Co. Ltd., and St. Martin's Press, Inc.
4. St. John 10:10.
5. Alec R. Vidler, *Christian Belief and This World*, Seabury Press, Greenwich, 1957.
6. From *The Witnessing Community*, by Suzanne de Dietrich, p. 16. Copyright 1958, by W. L. Jenkins. The Westminster Press. Used by permission.
7. G. D. Rosenthal, *Sins of the Saints*, Morehouse-Barlow Co., New York, 1958, p. 129.
8. Hymn No. 21, "O little town of Bethlehem," *The Hymnal* 1940.
9. Suzanne de Dietrich, *op. cit.*, p. 130.
10. Psalm 139:5-7, Book of Common Prayer.
11. David Elton Trueblood, *Philosophy of Religion*, Harper & Brothers, New York, 1957, p. 22.
12. From *The Power of Positive Thinking* by Norman Vincent Peale, © 1956 by Prentice-Hall, Inc., Englewood Cliffs, N. J., p. 100.
13. Emily Gardiner Neal, *A Reporter Finds God Through Spiritual Healing*, Morehouse-Barlow Co., New York, 1956.
14. St. Mark 5:34, St. Luke 8:48, 17:19.
15. II Corinthians 12:9.
16. Jude 3.
17. St. Matthew 7:14.

Letter XI

1. Rosemary Howard-Bennett, *I Choose the Cloister*, Hodder and Stoughton, Ltd., London, 1956, p. 12.

Letter XII

1. I Thessalonians 5:21.

DATE DUE

IDEAL 3370 UNGUMMED, 3371 GUMMED   PRINTED IN U.S.A.